GLOUCE

FOLK
TALES

GLOUCESTERSHIRE
FOLK
TALES

ANTHONY NANSON

The
History
Press

To Kirsty

First published 2012

The History Press
The Mill, Brimscombe Port
Stroud, Gloucestershire, GL5 2QG
www.thehistorypress.co.uk

Reprinted 2016

British Library Cataloguing in Publication Data.
A catalogue record for this book is available from the British Library.

ISBN 978 0 7524 6017 8

Typesetting and origination by The History Press
Printed in Great Britain

CONTENTS

ACKNOWLEDGEMENTS

I wish to acknowledge the sources listed in the Bibliography and the links in the chain by which the stories reached those publications. Where possible I've drawn on multiple sources for each story here retold. I thank Mike Rust for telling me 'The Wish Bottle' and 'The Bogglewort', and Kirsty Hartsiotis for sharing her concept of 'The Devil in Gloucestershire'. I also acknowledge Kirsty's telling of 'Mabon, Son of Modron', 'On Downham Hill' and 'The Painswick Elders' (and Robin Williamson's telling of a similar story), David Lowsley-Williams's 'The King's Revenge', Kevan Manwaring's 'Maude's Elm' and David Phelps's 'The Flying Pear Trees'. Many thanks also to Maggie Armstrong, Marec Barden, Elizabeth Cowen, Fiona Eadie, Laura Kinnear, Lisa Kopper, Caroline Lowsley-Williams, Kevan Manwaring, Rupert Matthews, David Metcalfe, Gabriel Millar, Simon Nanson, Glenn Smith, John Stevinson, Jess Wilson, Newent Storytellers, Bath Storytelling Circle, Stroud Library, Gloucestershire Archives, Bristol Central Library, and the History Press editors. Special thanks to David Phelps, who commented on the text and initiated this whole book series, and to Kirsty Hartsiotis, who helped me every step of the way and drew the marvellous illustrations.

MAP OF THE STORIES

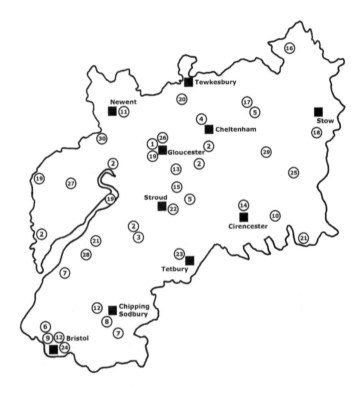

The numbers in the map refer to the numbering of the stories.

INTRODUCTION

Gloucestershire has good claim to be at the heart of Britain's history. The county sits at the boundaries between England and Wales and between Mercia and Wessex. The mouth of the Severn was of strategic importance from the Roman conquest to the Civil War and beyond. Rich farmland made this land of the native Dobunni the favoured location of Roman villas, forerunners of the manors and country houses of later centuries. The county was once crowded with vibrant monasteries, but also became a centre of Protestant reform. And the great port cities of Bristol and Gloucester have, throughout history, linked the local communities and landscapes of Forest, Vale and Wold to the wider world.

Although Gloucestershire has fewer well-shaped folk narratives than some counties, it is blessed with very many local legends that offer at least the potential for a good story. I was so spoilt for choice that I agonised over which stories to include. I've tried to provide a good spread of location, period and genre, and I've given priority to stories with a strong imaginative element as opposed to ones that are essentially a matter of recorded history. That was one reason for omitting the famous 'Campden Wonder'; it's also a peculiarly nasty story that I feel disinclined to inflict on a live audience.

Whereas a folklorist's job is to record and interpret folk tales as they find them, a storyteller has to make the tales shapely and satisfying to entertain an audience. Some stories in this collection I've simply retold in my own words; others I have considerably reshaped and elaborated. In some cases, I've linked together a number of related legends or scraps of folklore to make a longer, more structured story. In a few, I've drawn on versions of the same story from outside the county to fill out the Gloucestershire tale.

One interesting thing about local legends is that most of them have, at some point in time, been regarded as true history, and many involve real historical characters. They express an intersection between history and imagination, which requires the storyteller to make decisions about historical veracity. My approach is to treat this as a kind of puzzle in which I try to respect those historical facts which are known with conclusive certainty, but give free rein to tradition and imagination where there are gaps or uncertainties of knowledge. I'd add that, in talking to the owners of centuries-old houses and inns about the ghosts that haunt them, and in finding out about the big cats that have recently entered Gloucestershire folklore, I've seen that even in the twenty-first century local legends can continue to be persuasive as true history.

I've made a point of visiting all the Gloucestershire locations in these stories, in hopes thereby that my retellings will convey some sense of place. Where the sources didn't give an exact location, I scouted out a spot that seemed to fit. In some places the setting appears little changed since the time the story is set; in others it has changed dramatically. Gloucestershire's environment is in better shape than some counties', but even so the beauty and ecology of many localities are subject to pressures from urban development or industrialised agriculture. It's my belief that knowledge of traditional stories can impart an enchanted sense of significance to the landscapes and townscapes in which they're set. If the sharing of these Gloucestershire tales may contribute in some way to the appreciation of the county's specialness and a deeper caring for its communities and landscapes, then I shall be well pleased.

One

MABON, SON OF MODRON

Prince Culhwch was cursed by his stepmother with a tynged, or destiny, that the only woman he could ever marry was Olwen, daughter of the giant Ysbaddaden. Just to hear that name – 'Olwen' – was enough: Culhwch fell headlong in love.

'But Ysbaddaden is fiercely protective of his daughter,' said the stepmother, 'and with good reason. He knows that when she marries it will be his doom to die. He's hostile indeed to any suitor.'

Culhwch had no idea even where the giant and his daughter lived. But he had to have her! So he took his father's advice and went to Caerleon to ask a boon of his cousin, King Arthur.

'What boon do you wish?' said the High King.

'A haircut, sire, from your own hands.'

King Arthur called for comb and shears and there in his hall, before all the company of ladies and knights, he trimmed Culhwch's hair. As he did so, he deduced from the shape of the young man's skull that he must be his own kinsman.

'Tell me who you are!'

'I am Culhwch, son of Cilydd.'

'My cousin!' Arthur hugged him like a bear. 'Now I've cut your hair your destiny's in my care. Tell me your heart's desire and I shall see it won.'

'What I desire is the hand in marriage of Olwen, daughter of Ysbaddaden.'

The High King looked in silent entreaty to his henchmen. They rolled their eyes and shrugged.

'I've never heard of her, or her father,' he said, 'but if the lass exists, and is willing, I promise she will be yours.'

To undertake this quest Arthur called on his front bench of knights: Cei, who could hold his breath underwater for nine days and night nights; and Bedwyr, who, though he had only one hand, possessed a spear that with each thrust added nine more of its own; and Cynddylig, who could navigate as accurately in unknown lands as in his own; and Gwrhyr, who knew all the tongues of birds and beasts; and Gawain, who never returned from a quest without what he'd gone to seek; and Menw, who had the power to make himself and his companions invisible.

With Culhwch to complete their number, this magnificent seven searched the length and breadth of Britain until at last, on a wild windy plain grazed by an immense flock of sheep guarded by a mastiff as big as a stallion, they came to Ysbaddaden's castle. A huge hairy brute the giant was, with knotted greasy hair, and a beard crusted with the blood and brains of his daughter's suitors, and eyelids so wrinkled and heavy that his servants had to prop them up with staffs so he could see the visiting knights. Beside him his daughter was a paragon of proportion and elegance; I wish I had time to describe every detail of her beauty. If Culhwch already loved her from hearing her name, he loved her nine times more now he saw her in the flesh.

'I have come,' he said, when Gawain nudged him in the ribs, 'to ask for the hand in marriage of your daughter Olwen.'

From the way the girl's eyes shone, Culhwch could see she was willing. But Ysbaddaden knew that it was his doom to die when his daughter married. That was the way of things, harsh but true, only he wasn't ready to die yet.

'If you would marry my daughter, you must first bring me these things I ask' – and the giant enumerated a list of thirty-nine awesome tasks. To explain how marvellous was each thing he demanded, and how impossible to accomplish, would take hours. Only Gawain was still fully awake, making notes, when Ysbaddaden reached the thirty-ninth task: 'Finally you must give me a haircut. But my hair can only be shorn with the comb and shears that are lodged between the ears of Twrch Trwyth, greatest of all boars, and you'll never bring him to bay unless you have the hound Drudwyn, and Drudwyn can only be controlled with the leash of Cors Hundred-Claws, and that leash can only be held by the collar of Canhastyr Hundred-Hands, and that collar and that leash can only be linked by the chain of Cilydd Hundred-Holds. But even then no one can master Drudwyn in the chase except only Mabon, son of Modron, who was taken from his mother when he was three nights old and hasn't been seen since.'

When Culhwch was sure the giant had finished, he said, 'Not hard. I can do that,' and with a last glance at the beauteous Olwen he and his companions returned to Caerleon to devise a plan.

'Which task should we do first?' said Cei.

'Find Mabon,' said Gawain. 'If we can do that, we can do the rest.'

'Where shall we seek him?' asked Cynddylig, who was keen to start navigating.

The knights all looked at each other.

King Arthur said, 'Ask the Blackbird of Cilgwri. She's immensely old. If she doesn't know, I don't know who will.'

So the seven knights rode north to the Wirral to find this Blackbird. Gwrhyr, who knew all the tongues of beasts and birds, asked her, 'Can you tell us where to find Mabon, son of Modron, who was taken from his mother when he was three nights old and hasn't been seen since?'

The Blackbird indicated a nodule of iron on the ground, no bigger than a hazelnut. 'You see that? When I first came here, that was a great anvil. Once each day I wiped my beak on it and now this nodule is all that's left. That's how long I've been here, and I've never heard of Mabon. But there's one creature I know who's older than me. Ask the Stag of Rhedynfre. If he doesn't know, I don't know who will.'

The knights rode south to find the Stag on his ferny hill, and Gwrhyr asked him, 'Have you seen Mabon, son of Modron, who was taken from his mother when he was three nights old and hasn't been seen since?'

The Stag showed them a rotting stump of enormous girth. 'Since I came here I've seen an acorn grow into an oak with a thousand branches, and then wither away till all that remains is this stump. That's how long I've been here, and I've never heard of Mabon. But there is one I know who's older than me. Ask the Owl of Cwm Cawlwyd. If she doesn't know, I don't know who will.'

The knights rode west into Snowdonia and an oak-filled valley where they found the Owl.

'Can you tell us where to find Mabon, son of Modron, who was taken from his mother when he was three nights old and hasn't been seen since?'

The Owl stiffly stretched her wings. 'Since I came here I've seen bare heathland grow into a great forest and then, as the climate got dry, diminish into heath again, and then, as the climate became wet once more, I saw the forest regrow, and then once again I saw it disappear and a third time regrow. That's how long I've been here, and I've never heard of Mabon. But there's one creature I know who's older than me. Ask the Eagle of Gwernabwy. If he doesn't know, I don't know who will.'

The knights rode on into the mountains till they found the Eagle.

'Have you seen Mabon, son of Modron, who was taken from his mother when he was three nights old and hasn't been seen since?'

'You see that low bare knoll?' said the Eagle. 'When I first came here, that was a mountain, from whose summit I pecked at the stars. Grain by grain the wind and rain wore away that mountain till only this little knoll remains. That's how long I've been here, and I've never heard of Mabon.'

The knights looked at each other in despair. Even Gawain, who'd never returned from a quest without what he'd sought, was ready to call it a day.

'However …' said the Eagle, 'there is one I know who's even older than me. Ask the Salmon of Llyn Llyw. If he doesn't know where Mabon is, I'm sure that no one will.'

The knights returned south to Gwent and through the Forest of Dean to the river Lyd. In a deep pool fringed with trees of many kinds, not far from the Severn, they found that huge old Salmon.

'Can you tell us, O Salmon, where to find Mabon, son of Modron, who was taken from his mother when he was three nights old and hasn't been seen since?'

The Salmon pondered the question. 'I've been swimming between the ocean and the rivers since before the land was covered with ice and the sea froze, and I've never heard of Mabon … But I'll tell you something I do know. Each day I swim with the tide to Gloucester. Such things I've witnessed there as you'd never believe! From an island in the Severn stream I've heard a wailing woeful beyond imagining. If you have the courage to ride me I'll take you there to hear it.'

So the seven knights mounted the Salmon's scaly back and clung to his fins as he swam on the Severn's strong tide to the Roman walls of Gloucester. On an isle in the river's East Channel ancient stones lurked among the willows, and a woeful wailing shuddered through the earth as if to give vent to sorrows beyond sharing. Guarding the island's muddy shores were nine hideous women, in robes of black, with manes of grey hair straggling wild and knotted to their knees – the Nine Hags of Gloucester.

Culhwch's young voice called out clear as a bell, 'Who is that who wails?'

The answer came as if from a great distance and at the same time like a whisper in the ear: 'It is I, Mabon, son of Modron, and here I've been imprisoned a very long time.'

'How can you be freed?'

'By fighting.'

The seven knights drew their swords and leapt ashore. The Nine Hags lifted gnarled staffs to meet them. Fierce beyond belief were those hags in battle, testing the knights' courage, strength and skill to the utmost – till at last, when the knights thought they could fight no more, the women lowered their staffs and vanished like puffs of smoke. Amidst the dark willow stems, in the gap between two ancient stones, was a space like an eye upon its end, like the opening of a womb, rimmed with silver stars. Culhwch stepped as near as he dared and saw within those lips another world, with woods and streams and hills and sky, more brilliantly coloured than such things seem on this side. Encircled by nine women of unearthly beauty stood a young man whose features shone bright as the sun. When he stepped across the threshold between that world and this, everything around him became radiant and it seemed to Culhwch and his companions that all their hearts' deepest desires were possible.

With Mabon, son of Modron, they returned to Caerleon and set about the other tasks Ysbaddaden had set. If I were to tell you how they accomplished them all we'd be here for days. But at last thirty-eight tasks were done, and they'd won too the hound Drudwyn and the leash, collar and chain to control him. With King Arthur and all his knights and hounds, Culhwch sailed to Ireland on the one remaining quest – to win the comb and shears from between the ears of Twrch Trwyth.

A long chase the boar led them, through Ireland and across the sea and through Wales. If I were to name every place they nearly caught him you could draw a map of those countries. At last they drove him into the corner of land where the Wye meets the Severn. Yet again the boar eluded them and plunged into the broad brown Severn, the hounds led by Drudwyn snapping at his tail. Mabon spurred his steed into the water after him, close enough to snatch the shears from his brow, but before he could grab the comb too the beast was galloping up the muddy southern shore. Into Cornwall they pursued him, all the way to Land's End, where they cornered him again and at last Mabon whipped the comb from between his ears.

Bedwyr raised his nine-fold-thrusting spear. 'Let's make an end of the brute!'

'No, let him live!' cried Mabon.

And Twrch Trwyth leapt from the cliffs into the sea and the pack of hounds after him. Away they swam through the Atlantic waves, never to be seen again.

With the comb, shears and the other treasures they'd won, Culhwch returned with his companions to Ysbaddaden's castle on its wild windy plain. The servants propped up the giant's eyelids so he could take the inventory of his demands. When he saw that everything was there, he surrendered to the comb and shears that Culhwch plied to hack the knotted greasy hair from his scalp.

'Is your daughter now mine?' Culhwch said when it was done.

'She is. But don't thank me. Thank King Arthur because you'd never have won her without the help he gave you. Now do to me what you must!'

Gawain handed Culhwch the axe and the young prince chopped off the giant's head. Olwen pressed her hand in his and everyone cheered, and when that night the prince and the giant's daughter became one flesh, it was as if two halves of the world that had been sundered had at last been rejoined.

Two

The Devil in Gloucestershire

'As sure as God's in Gloucestershire'; that's what they kept saying. It's true, there was an awful lot of God in Gloucestershire: all those churches and abbeys and saints. The Devil really wasn't happy about that. As he saw it, there needed to be a bit more Devil in Gloucestershire. It was a question of balance.

So out he shot from the hot place down below and landed in a corner of Gloucestershire – in Tidenham Chase. No sooner did he arrive, steaming in the cool damp woods, than who should appear but his old mate Jacky Kent? Thick in the thigh and thick in the arm, with curly hair and a cheerful grin, Jacky had his home in Herefordshire – but some say the Forest of Dean was once part of Herefordshire, so maybe he thought the Devil was trespassing on his patch.

The two of them had a pact from years ago that they could challenge each other to contests. So Jacky says, 'Let's have a stone-throwing contest.'

'You're on,' says the Devil, who was pretty good at throwing stones.

They found a spot at the edge of the trees where they could see down over the Severn. It all looked so peaceful and the

Devil thinks, 'What they need right there by the beach is a
nice big nuclear reactor. That will spice things up. Even better,
maybe two.'

Then he lifted a great stone and hurled it, sailing end over end
through the air, to land – smack! – in a field near the riverbank; a
good mile and a half.

'Not bad,' says Jacky.

Now, Jacky's a bit cleverer than he looks. He chose a stone
quite a bit smaller than the Devil's – there'd been no stipulation
about size – and whizzed it in a high arc clear across the river,
to land by a village they today call Stone in honour of this feat.
He'd beaten the Devil by a good three miles; his stone was so far
away – and so small – that you couldn't see it. Not like the Devil's
Quoit, jutting up proudly from the field. You can see it there still,
right next to the railway.

The Devil was pretty irked that Jacky had got the better of him again. He stamped off through the woods in search of something to cheer him up. He didn't have to go far. From the steep scarp along the Wye he could see down through a gap in the trees to Tintern Abbey – a dreary-looking place where the monks were going about their tedious little lives like ants. The Devil built himself a fine rocky pulpit on which he could easily be seen, and set about waving his arms and howling at the top of his voice to distract the monks from their devotions.

After a time he got bored with that, and Tintern wasn't in Gloucestershire anyway, so he left the Devil's Pulpit where it stands to this day, and wandered on to see what other mischief he could do. Right across the Forest he went. 'Dreadful place! Too many trees everywhere! I ought to get the place sold off to someone who'll chop them all down.'

What annoyed him as well was the way his toenails, which he'd neglected to trim and had grown into claws, kept catching on the undergrowth. When he reached the Severn, he sat down with his back against Hock Cliff and hacked off the ends of his toenails with a stone. He left the parings scattered at the foot of the cliff. It entertained him in later years when earnest fellows came to collect these Devil's toenails, believing them to be the remains of a prehistoric oyster, and displayed them in cabinets for public scrutiny.

The Devil traipsed on to Westbury-on-Severn. He was still vexed about Jacky Kent having beaten him so badly, and bothered that he hadn't achieved much yet. So when he saw the spire of Westbury Church reaching up towards heaven and heard the people inside singing praises to God, he yelled in anger, 'I'll teach them!' and grabbed the spire in both hands, and with a sharp twisting motion pulled the whole tower away from the rest of the church and planted it on the ground a short distance away. It looks a bit odd, and if you stare up from the bottom you can still see the twist in the spire, but it didn't stop the people praying.

'What would be fun', thinks the Devil, 'would be a civil war, with soldiers from one side holed up in the tower and those of the other side shooting at them from the church.' He rubbed his hands in glee. And on he went.

He steered clear of Gloucester and its great abbey. There was a scary lot of God in there. Gloucester had potential, though. 'What it needs is some big roads, where people will try to drive fast, and some confusing bits where there's more chance they'll crash or get enraged.' Some day he'd get round to it.

He climbed up to the northern edge of Leckhampton Hill, where there's a grand view across the Vale and he could see pilgrims making their way through Cheltenham towards Hailes Abbey. Cheltenham wasn't much of a place then; the Devil had plans for Cheltenham too, but right now it was Hailes that troubled him. God really was in Gloucestershire there: they had a phial of Christ's blood, authenticated by the Pope, on display in a fancy shrine, which attracted legions of pilgrims to come and pray. So the Devil ripped up rocks from the edge of the hill and pelted them at the pilgrims as they passed within range. Excellent sport! He'd have gladly carried on doing that quite a while, but one big rock was quite deeply embedded and when at last he tugged it free the edge of the hill collapsed under him. Down he fell, to the bottom, and an avalanche of rocks tumbled down and buried him.

So there was the Devil, buried under tons of rock, and he was furious; he was so angry that he fumed and stewed and simmered and hot gases belched out of him with such force that a chimney grew from the rubble, higher and higher, belching steam and smoke like a volcano, till the Devil shot right out of the top of that Devil's Chimney, did a triple somersault in the air, over Leckhampton Hill, over Crickley Hill, and landed on his head on Birdlip Hill.

He was feeling really angry now, and thirsty, and his head hurt, and he hated how quiet and calm it was around this hill. 'Ought to build a really noisy dual carriageway through here to give the place some character.' Some day he'd find time to get these things done; but very soon he had to get back down to the hot place. Responsibilities, you know: admin; management. It would, though, be good to take a soul or two as recompense for all his efforts up here. And he was nation thirsty – yes, damnation thirsty – after getting buried under those rocks. So when in the fading light he saw a shepherd heading down from Birdlip, towards the inn at Little Witcombe, the Devil rubbed his hands. He bided his time; best strike when it was dark and the bloke would likely be carrying some booze to nourish him when he got back to his sheep.

One of those sheep, as it chanced, had some nasty sores. The shepherd's purpose at the inn was to get some strong medicine to use on those sores. He bought a hornful of ale too, which he sipped as he returned along the track. It was dark, but he knew the way. As he came to the turning into Dog Lane, just before the track turns up Birdlip Hill, he heard the melancholy howl of the black dog that haunts that lane. The shepherd knew that the dog meant well. The howl could be a warning. He took another bib of ale to fortify his nerves. It was a shame to waste good ale, but better safe than sorry: he tipped a bit of the sheep medicine into the horn and continued up the track.

Out of the darkness loomed a stocky figure with a mirthless scowl. The shepherd recoiled in fear. The Devil was quick, he grabbed him by the arms, and his hot smelly breath hissed in the man's face. 'Will you give me some ale to quench my thirst?'

The shepherd handed over the horn – 'Spiced special for you, sir' – and legged it as fast as he could run.

The Devil was so thirsty he quaffed the ale in one gulp. When it hit the back of his throat he roared so loud you could hear him in Cheltenham.

Foiled again! The Devil was still raging, still groaning with pain, when he got to Painswick. All those yews in the churchyard, how he hated them, cloaking the whole place with such tedious sanctity! He did a quick count. Someone had planted a hundredth one! Even worse! He pulled up the new yew. Back to ninety-nine. 'With any luck, some day they'll all die and then I'll get to business here.'

By now the Devil was feeling really angry with Gloucestershire and all the God that still was in it despite all his efforts.

Drastic measures were called for. 'I'm going to dam the Severn so the water will back up and flood the whole Vale. That'll teach them!' He got a big wheelbarrow and, just above Uley, loaded it with earth. Then he trundled it down towards the river. He hadn't got far and he was feeling tired and time was getting short when he met a cobbler coming the other way with a sack of old shoes on his back.

'How far is it to the Severn?' asks the Devil.

The cobbler regarded this big fellow with his browsy scowling face and steam hissing from his nostrils. He pulled a shoe from the sack and pointed out the hole that had worn right through the sole.

'You see that? I wore out this shoe walking all this way from the Severn.'

'It must be a heck of a distance,' thinks the Devil. 'I don't have time to push a wheelbarrow all that way.' He upended the wheelbarrow right there and the earth made a huge big conical mound – which has stayed there ever since. They call it Cam Peak.

The Devil really thought he had something with that idea of damming the Severn. Maybe a tidal barrage would do the trick. But he really did have to be going.

Just then he got a message, by a devilish device of his devising, that at Berkeley, very near, there was a woman who'd lived a racy life and was now sick and about to die. She was a cunning woman too; she'd thought up a way to stop the Devil taking her soul.

'We'll see about that!' says the Devil.

Three

ON DOWNHAM HILL

Dusk comes early in the winter. The traveller, on his way from Bristol to see friends in Stroud, misjudged how far he had to ride, how much daylight was left. He was just past Dursley and night was falling when it began to snow, a fine dust at first, but soon the flakes fell bigger. The roads in those days were not what they are today, even the main roads were no more than dirt tracks, and in the darkness and thickening snow the traveller took a wrong turn. The Stroud road, he knew, climbed up to the scarp edge and followed it, but here he seemed to be among a huddle of hills rising on all sides into the falling snow. Modest downs they'd have looked in the sunshine, but at night, in this snowstorm, they might have been a highland wilderness. The mare skidded and stumbled on the slippery track. The man didn't know whether to head forwards or back. Soon he could no longer make out where the road was. A panic began to grip him inside as tight as the cold gripped his face. He'd nothing to shelter him except his hat and cloak. He could feel the icy slither down his spine of melting snow that had caught in his collar.

Then in the darkness he saw a light: a little beacon of yellow, blurred through the snowflakes. It appeared at first to be in the sky, so steep was the hill from which it shone. To the traveller it seemed his only hope. He could find no path up that hill. He had to lead his horse on foot, scrambling and slithering up slippery dead bracken, till he saw a stand of trees. Through their bare branches the lantern shone from a gable window. When he reached the hill crest he saw light gleaming from a ground-storey window too ... and then from the doorway as the door swung open.

He stepped with relief into the inn's cosy warmth, where a fire crackled in the hearth and the smell of stewed mutton teased his nostrils. The groom who'd opened the door, a wizened little chap cloaked in green, stepped out without a word and led the horse to the stable. The traveller crouched by the fire to thaw his bones. He noticed how empty the inn seemed; and silent.

Out to the stable he went to check on the mare. He found her tucking into a sack of oats and the groom rubbing the wet snow from her hide.

'Thank you,' the traveller said.

The groom glanced up with mirthless eyes that looked as though they'd seen every winter since England began.

Back inside the inn, the place seemed as empty as before, no sound except the crackling of the fire ... till the traveller heard a creaking of floorboards above his head. He ventured upstairs and came face to face with a servingwoman, one who seemed neither young nor old, who was dressed all in green and regarded him with impassive grey eyes. She showed him to a room where a fire was lit and mulled ale was warming in a jug beside it and a dish of stew and dumplings waiting on a stool. She took his cloak and jacket and pulled off his snow-stiffened boots.

'Thank you,' said the traveller, and without a word the woman carried the wet garments away.

He muttered thanks to God too. It was hard to believe that only minutes before he'd been lost in the snowstorm and had, truth be told, slim hope of surviving the night. Gratefully he ate the stew, drank the ale, and warmed his undergarments by the fire. Soon the food, the ale, the warmth, his tiredness got the better of him. He fell into bed and slept.

He woke, an hour before dawn, to an uncanny stillness. He knew by the glimmer of starlight between the shutters that the snowing had stopped. In the ruddy glow from the hearth he saw his boots standing clean and dry, and his cloak and jacket draped neatly over the chair. On the stool was a plate of bread and cheese, and by the fire a new jug of ale.

The traveller knew that his friends in Stroud would be worried he'd not made it through the snowstorm last night. He knew what he should do: get started right away, to get to their house as soon as he could to put their minds at rest. But it would be freezing outside, this hour before dawn. Why not stay under these toasty blankets, sleep a while longer, till the sun was up? Surely another hour or two would make little difference to John and Annie's fretting. As he debated this, he was struck once again by the inn's silence. What business could the landlord hope to do here, on top of a hill, away from any coach route?

Fully awake now, the traveller felt his conscience prick sharper. Time to get up! He rinsed his face, put on his clothes, and gobbled up his breakfast. There was no one about downstairs, neither landlord, nor servant, nor guest. Empty chairs behind empty tables. The fire's embers smouldered in the hearth.

Outside, the night air was shiveringly crisp and chill. Silver starlight illuminated the black sycamores beside the inn and

the swell and hollow of the hills and valleys below, all blanketed with snow. The traveller went to the stable to saddle the mare, then slipped back into the inn to find someone to pay. There was still no one about. He was reluctant to call out lest he wake any sleeping guests. Yet it seemed for all the world that he was the only mortal soul in that place.

What to do? He took two gold guineas from his purse and placed them on a table.

'That should be enough.'

He led the mare carefully down the snow-crusted slope. At the bottom they picked up a bridleway that, to judge by the Pole Star, led north-east. It took them steeply up to one end of the rampart-ringed camp of Uley Bury and the road along the escarpment, past prehistoric barrows, spooky swellings of earth in the dawn's pink light.

The sun was long risen before the traveller reached Stroud. He was yet some distance from his friends' house when he saw two riders coming his way: John Hayward and his handsome green-eyed Annie.

'Thank the good Lord to see you!' cried John.

'We prayed you'd not tried to come through the snowstorm,' said Annie.

The traveller made a rueful face. 'The snow caught me asaddle, but providence brought me to a fine inn on a hill above Dursley.'

'An inn above Dursley? On a hill?' John Hayward shook his head. 'There's no inn around there.'

'There most certainly was!' The traveller told them what fine hospitality he'd received.

'It must be Downham Hill.' Annie had that sparkle in her eyes. 'I've told you before, John, I've heard tell of an inn there.'

'If that's the case, my dear, and as the two of you appear to be in league against me, I would be very glad to see this inn.'

So with his friends the traveller rode back along the escarpment. They retraced the mare's hoofprints in the snow to the foot of Downham Hill. There they tethered the horses to a tree and John Hayward said to his wife, 'Perhaps you'd stay and keep watch on the horses? This hill looks a mite steep and slippery for a gentlewoman.'

'I'm not staying down here after I've come all this way!' Annie lifted her skirts and gamely followed the two men up the trail of hoofprints.

'It's just behind the trees,' said the traveller, eager to make his point.

They crested the hilltop. There were the trees. Their skeletal branches concealed nothing. Beyond was only the white surface of snow, in which a few hollows and lumps spoke of excavations in some bygone time.

'But it was here!' The traveller ran forward and with a stabbing finger indicated the exact position of the inn with respect to the trees. 'Right here!' The hoofprints led all the way to where the stable door had been.

'Well,' said John Hayward, not quite sure what to think, 'it looks like I was right …'

'Look!' Annie pointed at a spot on the ground a few yards from the traveller's feet.

The traveller looked down. Glittering bright in the snow were two gold coins.

'Those are my guineas! The payment I left on the table!'

'They never take payment, so I've heard,' said Annie. 'It's on stormy nights they like to come out, but they never stay after sunrise.' She turned to the traveller and gave him her sparkling green gaze. 'It's just as well you got up early. Otherwise you'd have woken to find yourself lying in the snow … if you'd woken up at all.'

Four

MAUDE'S ELM

Swindon Village is today an industrial suburb of Cheltenham, but an area of woods and older buildings near the church gives an inkling of what the place was like years ago, when Cheltenham itself was little more than a village. In a thatched cottage beside the churchyard, a lovely young woman called Maude Bowen once lived with her mother, Margaret. They made a meagre living by spinning. One spring day, Maude carried a bundle of yarn to sell in Cheltenham, as she'd often done before. By nightfall she'd not returned and Margaret got worried. She called out her neighbours and they searched the lanes, the woods, the Cheltenham road; they searched all night without any trace of Maude, till shortly after dawn they found her floating face-down in the still dark water of Wymans Brook, her long brown hair twisting in the eddies, her clothes in disarray. On the footbridge nearby lay the body of her uncle, Godfrey Bowen, with an arrow through his heart and Maude's torn mantlet in his stiffened hands.

Everyone had their own ideas about what had happened, but the view of Sir Robert de Vere, the lord of the manor, was that Godfrey had raped the girl, God had punished him, and Maude had drowned herself in shame. Sir Robert insisted the letter of the law must be obeyed – 'For suicide is a crime against God.' Godfrey, being slain by God, was buried in the churchyard, whereas Maude was buried in unconsecrated ground outside the village, at dead of night, without ceremony or sacred words, with an elm stake through her heart to ensure her unshriven shade would not haunt the living.

The villagers were appalled. Maude was a kind girl, whom everyone had loved, and surely the victim in this tragedy. Sir Robert had his reasons. Maude's offence against God gave him an excuse to evict her ageing mother from the cottage and move in a family who could pay more rent. Devastated by grief, and homeless, with nowhere to do her spinning, poor Margaret lived as a vagrant, begging scraps from the villagers. They say she went insane. She spent long hours at her daughter's grave by the Cheltenham road, always weeping, so her tears watered the stake they'd driven through Maude's heart, till the stake took root and put forth a shoot, which budded leaves and began to grow. Years went by, endlessly Margaret wept at that spot, and the sapling grew into an elegant young elm, slender and lovely as the woman from whose body it had grown.

One day, after Sir Robert de Vere had been blessed with a baby son, he came by from the christening with his wife and child in the carriage and a troop of retainers on foot. As they passed the elm, the air was rent by old Margaret's inconsolable sobs. Lady de Vere looked up aghast, the baby wailed, and Sir Robert was furious that his happy day should be disturbed.

'Remove that hag from here!' he ordered one of his men.

When the servant tried to drag her, Margaret resisted with a vigour surprising in a woman so worn down by poverty, grief and age. Suddenly, from a hawthorn thicket, an arrow sped, and pierced the man through the heart – and down he fell, stone dead. Sir Robert roared and raged. His men searched the thicket, and the fields and woods beyond, but no archer could be found.

'In the name of God,' Sir Robert accused the old woman, 'it is by foul witchcraft that you conjured an arrow to slay my servant!'

On that weighty charge, Margaret was taken to Gloucester Gaol. A few weeks locked up in the darkness and squalor took a swift toll on her body and mind. When they put her on trial she could hardly stand to face the charges. She could string together no words to answer them. By Sir Robert's eloquent evidence she was found guilty of witchcraft and sentenced to be bound to the unholy elm that had nourished her evil powers and there burnt, that God's earth might be cleansed at a stroke of both woman and tree.

So it was done, and when the flames took hold of Margaret Bowen's clothes and she began to scream, Sir Robert jeered and laughed. 'May you burn in hell forever – you and your accursed daughter!'

The words had no sooner left his lips than an arrow sped from the hawthorns, straight through his heart, and he tumbled headlong into the flames. The fire burst into a blazing inferno. The spectators leapt back from the heat. Margaret's screams were engulfed by the roaring flames. In minutes the bodies of both woman and lord were consumed.

Yet the elm survived the fire, for Sir Robert's men added no more fuel and the flames soon burnt themselves out. The tree's bark was badly charred, but the heartwood was intact; the tree stood firm. A new lord took the manor. The elm grew and grew. Fifty years passed and it became a tall, stately tree. The Bowen cottage lay abandoned and in ruins, when a wild-haired old man came to live there. No one bothered him; he kept to himself and was often seen sitting in sad contemplation beside the elm. He gave away nothing about his past till at last his strength began to fail and he knew his time was nigh. Then at last he told his story to those who would listen.

'My name – my real name – was Walter Gray. I once aspired to be a poet, though I had to toil in the fields like the next man. There's no one left alive in this village who'll remember me. I was the same age as Maude Bowen. I'd loved her since I was a child, and she loved me, and we were going to be wed just as soon as I had some money. I used to practise my skill with the bow in hopes I might win some prizes.

'The thing is' – the old man shivered with distaste – 'her uncle Godfrey had taken a fancy to her, though he knew he could never marry her. Maude always had to have her wits about her to fend off his advances. When she was twenty she told him outright he must desist, as she was an honest woman and engaged to be married. He knew then he had no chance of her. If his soul was already rotten, now it festered worse. He noticed that his lordship also had a fancy for young Maude and was biding the chance to take his pleasure of her. So Godfrey went to Sir Robert, in hopes of his favour and to punish Maude for spurning him, and offered to put her in his lordship's power.

'That evening, Maude and I had arranged to meet on the bridge. If only I'd got there first! I was coming through the woods when I heard her voice disputing with someone and uttering little screams, as if in distress but not wanting to be heard. I quickened my step, and through the may leaves I saw her wrestling with Godfrey on the bridge. I heard her shout, "No!" I had to do something. I had my bow, so I nocked an arrow and when his chest was clear as a bullseye above her I let fly. Down went he. Maude pushed free and raced off through the willows by the brook. I started after her, called her name. She didn't reply. I thought maybe she'd had such a shock she wanted to be alone or else get home to her mama.

'That was my mistake. I can never forgive myself I didn't carry right on after her – not till I heard through the trees a yelp of surprise, like you make when you trip, and then the splash, and more splashing, someone struggling and gasping in the water. It was dark under the willows; there were brambles to fight through. By the time I got there it was too late, she'd drowned, and I tell you it was no suicide.

'When I heard people coming near, I was afraid. I'd killed a man and who knows what they might think if they found me there with a drowned woman. So I ran away. I fled from Swindon. I changed my name. I grew my hair and beard long. But I didn't go far – only to Hayden, where I ended up landlord of the inn. I kept an eye on Margaret Bowen when I could. It was me who shot his lordship's man when he tried to drag her away from Maude's grave. It was me who shot Sir Robert himself when he mocked her as she burned.'

That was Walter Gray's tale. When he died, they buried him the only place he wanted to be, at the foot of the elm, united at last with the one he'd loved. And still the tree grew, till it was eighty feet high, a majestic great elm rising from the junction of three roads. In the eighteenth century, when Cheltenham became fine and grand, the gentry would ride out in their carriages to view that veteran tree.

In 1907 the elm was struck by lightning, declared unsafe, and chopped down. Today there's just a mini-roundabout at the spot where it stood. The place seems forgotten, neglected, built up all the way into Cheltenham. It would be a fine thing to plant a young elm in memory of the old one, but these days, of course, it wouldn't grow very tall before Dutch elm disease took it. All that's left to mark this tragic tale is a little sign on the wall which says, 'Maude's Elm'.

Five

THE BISLEY BOY

In the year 1543, when the young Lady Elizabeth was feeling off-colour, her attendants took her to Overcourt, a manor house that had once been her mother's, in Bisley, high in the Cotswolds. The pure air would do her good, they thought. Word came that the King was coming to see his nine-year-old daughter. That in itself was enough to put Elizabeth's governess, Kat Champernowne, and steward, Thomas Parry, into a flap. But a few days before the King was due to arrive, Elizabeth's illness became a raging fever – typhoid – and she died.

Thomas and Kat grieved for the little girl, whom they'd loved, but they were in terror for their lives. The daughter of Henry VIII had died in their care! They kept the death secret from the servants, the villagers, from everyone. In dead of night they moved the body to an old stone coffin hidden in the undergrowth in the manor grounds. All they could think of was the King's impending visit. Henry didn't see his daughter often; there was a chance he could be deceived. They searched for a girl of similar age and appearance, but there was none in Bisley who remotely resembled Elizabeth – and no time to look further afield.

'If we can't find a girl,' Kat whispered to Thomas, 'then why not a boy?'

'A boy?'

'There is a boy who in every respect except his sex would be perfect.'

She meant Neville, the illegitimate son of the King's own illegitimate son, Henry Fitzroy. Being an embarrassment to everyone − Fitzroy had sired him at the age of thirteen − the boy had been farmed out to a spinster cousin of his mother's hidden away in Bisley. He was the same age as Elizabeth to within a month, and shared her sallow-skinned, red-haired looks. He'd romped with her in the gardens and orchards, and he'd been well tutored, to have a chance in the world even if his parentage were secret.

Thomas Parry went to fetch him, then went back to speak frankly to the boy's guardian, and the tutor, and one elderly servant. 'For the high purposes of the realm, I bid you put this boy from your mind as if he never existed; I bid you never to speak of him or his departure from this house. On pain of death I so enjoin you.'

Kat Champernowne made a game of dressing Neville in Elizabeth's clothes and instructing him how to deport himself like a princess. 'The King is coming to see his daughter and we must not disappoint him. Elizabeth is … gone − and the King mustn't know − so you must be Elizabeth. Do you think you can do that?'

Neville was a clever lad and amused by the part he was asked to play. The big day came. He rose in his skirts to curtsey as the King's vast bulk filled the panelled parlour. Thomas and Kat watched in breathless terror as Henry peered down over his corseted belly and lifted the child's chin with one meaty finger.

'Upon my word, Elizabeth, you do remind me of myself at your age. I wasn't always fat, you know.' He tested the child's arms. 'What a fine strong lass you are! 'Tis a shame you're not a boy, because then you'd be king after me − and that, I can tell you, would save me much vexation.'

Thomas and Kat let themselves breathe as Henry left the room. Neville played his part without a slip till the visit was over. But what was to be done next? To keep up the deception, or to stage a version of Elizabeth's death that would let Thomas and Kat off the hook? They never really made a decision. The situation just carried on as it was. So long as it did, Kat impressed upon the boy, he must reveal his true self to no one. So Neville became 'Elizabeth'. Her tutor noticed an improvement in his pupil's knowledge of ancient languages, Elizabeth having previously been a mediocre scholar. Others noticed an improvement of her teeth, which had been rotted by her liking for sweets. But no one suspected the extraordinary transformation hidden beneath her clothes.

Except perhaps one person. Upon marrying the King that same year of 1543, Catherine Parr treated Elizabeth with warmth and kindness as if she were her own daughter. When Henry died, Queen Catherine became the girl's guardian and when, with unseemly haste, Catherine married her old flame Sir Thomas Seymour, she took Elizabeth – and Kat, the devoted governess – to live with them in Sudeley Castle, near Winchcombe. Seymour was a charmer all right, but he was ambitious too. Catherine was too distracted by her own pregnancy to think what intentions lay behind his flirtation with her fourteen-year-old stepdaughter. Some mornings he came into Elizabeth's room, still in his nightclothes, while she was yet in bed. She'd leap up to wrestle him with surprising strength. Sometimes Catherine caught them at it. You might expect she'd be outraged, but instead she egged them on like a gambler at a prizefight. Seymour, if he'd stopped to think, might have wondered why his wife laughed so long and hard.

Kat Ashley – as Kat had become by marriage – was horrified. One too fierce tug at Elizabeth's shift and the truth would be revealed. To Catherine she came in private. 'Forgive me for speaking so bold, mam, but it greatly troubles me to see how Sir Thomas carries on with Elizabeth.' In Catherine's eyes she perceived an understanding she'd never seen in any other's save Thomas Parry's. 'O mam, as you love her, you will protect her from any danger?'

'Fear not, Kat. I love her as my own child.'

A few days later Catherine chanced upon her husband and Elizabeth, not wrestling, but holding each other in a close embrace. Over the man's shoulder Elizabeth looked into Catherine's eyes and the girl's face was filled with such a mixture of confusion and fear. Catherine put an end to things then and sent Elizabeth to London. But it was only briefly an end. Not long afterwards, Catherine gave birth to a daughter, childbed fever set in, and the Queen Dowager died. Freed from the constraint of marriage, Seymour pursued Elizabeth in London. He advanced a suit to marry her, which she rejected at once. He would not give up. Marriage to Henry's younger daughter was but part of his plan to win supreme power in England while the new king was yet a child. In that ambition he soon overstepped the mark and lost his head for his pains.

Meanwhile, Elizabeth was growing up. Only Kat Ashley had full access to her boudoir. No servant was allowed to see her body uncovered. She wore chest-flattening bodices to conceal that she had no bosom to flatten. She wore thick white make-up, full of lead, to hide the five o'clock shadow on her chin. She deployed a vast array of wigs to conceal her swiftly receding hairline.

Then young King Edward VI became sick. It was plain he was going to die. Now the stakes of everything were raised. Discovery would not only mean the death of the impostor and the two people who'd put him where he was, but also remove from the succession the Protestant heir who waited next in line after her sister, the Lady Mary, who was an ardent Roman Catholic and unable to bear a child. The future of England hung in the balance. So Thomas Parry sent men to Bisley to do what had to be done to ensure those few who knew about Elizabeth's secret would never speak of it. The spinster cousin, the tutor and the old servant vanished without trace. The people of Bisley, if they knew anything, took the point and breathed not a word.

In 1553 King Edward died and the whirlwind came: the nine-day reign of Lady Jane, the crowning of Mary, the Wyatt rebellion against the rise of Catholic power. Elizabeth was imprisoned in the Tower of London. There she fell ill, and her sister, the Queen, sent a doctor.

'I will have no doctor prodding and poking me,' said Elizabeth. 'My body I commend to the mercy of God.'

God was merciful, Elizabeth got well, and through the bloodbath of Mary's reign the secret was kept. No doctor ever examined Elizabeth. No lover ever caressed her. So it continued when she became queen. She played the diplomatic game of entertaining suitors from Europe's royal courts, but she knew all along she could never marry. She made Kat Ashley the first lady of the bedchamber and Thomas Parry the comptroller of the household and was loyal to them always. She ruled forty-four years, Good Queen Bess, the beloved ruler of England's Golden Age. When at last the lead in her make-up had taken its toll, even then when she was dying, she let no doctor near her. She tried to die standing on her feet, till at last, too weak, she had to lie down. She commanded there should be no post-mortem and took her secret to her grave in Westminster Abbey.

The people of Bisley remained silent. But they knew, of course. How could they not in such a close-knit village? They never forgot the Bisley boy; their May queen was a boy dressed like a Tudor-period girl. When, in 1880, foundations for a school were being dug on land from Overcourt, a stone coffin was discovered. Under the supervision of the vicar, Thomas Keble, the workmen heaved off the lid to discover inside the remains of a young girl wearing a beautiful silk gown of the sixteenth century. At last the story came out. Keble wouldn't disclose where he reburied the body, but it's said the real Elizabeth Tudor lies buried a couple of miles north of Bisley in the Dillay Valley.

Six

THE SKY SHIP

It's always a fearful time, a fisherman's farewell to his wife when he sets out to sea. Before sunrise that morning, when Bertie Ashton had to go fishing even though it was the Sabbath, Alice hugged him tight on the Bristol quayside and watched him row his little boat down to the Avon on the ebbing tide. It was not wise to go alone to sea, but Bertie had no brother or partner to go with, and fish had to be caught to pay the rent and put food on the table.

There was mist on the Severn Sea that morning. As the sun rose, the mist thickened and Bertie lost sight of the shore. He took down the sail and rode the tide and prayed God would keep him off the rocks. The mist got so dense he couldn't even see the water right beside the boat. Only the sun's glow through the greyness told him he was heading west. How fast, how far west, he couldn't tell. He imagined his little craft getting carried out into the ocean. All he could do was pray.

The misty air got colder. Strangely, it got thinner too; so thin that Bertie couldn't find the breath to speak his prayers. He felt too breathless and dizzy to pull the oars even if he'd known which direction to row. His eyes fluttered closed …

Then he felt soft hands lifting him – and opened his eyes to behold slim-faced people, with big grey eyes and shimmering pale skin, and dressed in a diaphanous fabric that floated round their slender figures. Whether men or women, he wasn't sure. They lifted him aboard a ship partly obscured by the mist. The sails were huge, of a similar gauzy material, sunshine dazzling through. From smooth rounded cabins bright lights shone like fire. As the crew peered down at Bertie, they murmured in fluting birdlike voices he couldn't understand. He felt too weak to fight off their soft probing fingers. He wondered if he'd died and these strange beings were angels transporting him to heaven.

The fog cleared from around the vessel. Deep blue sky above. Far below, through wispy strands of cloud, was the textured surface of the sea. Bertie felt a hollow reeling inside his belly. This ship was sailing through the sky! Craning over the side, he saw a white-waved rim of land approaching, then green fields and woods, the winding ribbon of a river, and a city wall and bristling rooftops and steeples. Bristol! He could see the fishermen's shacks near the river. His own cottage was down there!

The sky ship's crew hauled at the great sails. The vessel swung in a broad arc towards the north. Bertie knew he had to act right now. It might be his only chance. Gasping to find breath, he lurched to his feet. The beings around him uttered little cries of what sounded like joy. He staggered between them to the anchor in the stern. Summoning all his strength, he heaved it over the side. Down the anchor plunged, its cord unreeling behind it. He reached to grasp the cord so as to plummet down with it, but soft strong hands restrained him. He pulled his knife from his belt. Its blade sliced the air and the sky sailors let out whistling gasps. Bertie's head was spinning. Someone caught him from behind, the knife was flung from his hand and over the side, and then he passed out.

At that same moment, Alice was brushing out the fireplace in their little cottage. She heard a clattering in the louvre overhead and – thunk! – a knife fell point first into the tabletop and stuck there, quivering. She looked up at the sunlight shining through the slots in the louvre. She looked back at the knife. It seemed familiar. She tugged it from the wooden tabletop. In the haft were carved the initials 'A.A.'

A few miles north-west, in St Mary's Church, Henbury, a visiting friar was preaching about the celestial realm – 'home of angels and archangels, of cherubim and seraphim, who look down upon our toils and cares, who watch over us, and when our time is come will take us to that higher realm where the Lord God will measure the worth of all that we have done'. The friar had more imagination than the parish priest; as the congregation spilled out from the church, blinking in the sunlight, their minds were alight with visions of a greater world. Then they blinked again, in astonishment, as a ship's anchor swung through the air on the end of a cord hanging from the sky. With a clang the anchor struck a cross-shaped gravestone, caught fast under its bar, and the rope strained steep into the sky. The people gazed up, but all they could see was the pattern of cloud and sunlight and blue firmament.

The friar, being a sharp-eyed fellow, spotted something descending the cord: a slender figure, whose diaphanous garment shimmied in the wind, who moved more and more laboriously the lower down the cord he – or she – came. Upon reaching the anchor, this shimmering being struggled to free it from the gravestone, but the rope was stretched too taut, and the sky being was visibly suffering, its face turning green, its mouth working at the air like someone drowning. It abandoned the anchor, made a feeble attempt to climb back up the cord, then sank to the ground, spasmed, and lay still – yet not exactly still, for the body began to collapse in on itself as if something were sucking it from inside.

Suddenly the anchor dropped from the grave cross, and the severed cord sinuously descended through the air. A gust of wind and the sky being's gown fragmented into shreds of nothingness. All that was left of the body was a shrivelled green husk. Some of the witnesses thought that they'd seen a miraculous confirmation of the friar's sermon. Others pondered whether it indicated quite the contrary, that the heavens were populated by mortal beings just as the earth was. Both those thoughts had occurred to the friar, and other thoughts too. On balance, it seemed to him for the best that this being from the sky had shrivelled into a shapeless husk.

It was some time later that Bertie became conscious of shining faces peering at him, soft hands gripping him, as the sky sailors lowered him from their ship. He heard the sloshing of waves. He felt under his back the wooden thwarts of his boat as it bobbed on the swell. Through the mist he glimpsed the golden light in the western sky, the darkness rising in the east. He was alone again at the mercy of wind and tide and wave. The mist thinned as the darkness thickened; he saw the faint yellow lights of farms to both starboard and larboard, the Welsh and Somerset coasts. He realised he could breathe well enough and his strength was back. He hoisted sail to harness the south-westerly wind blowing up the Channel, till he found the Avon's mouth, then rowed back to Bristol in the starlight.

'O Bertie!' cried Alice when he got home. 'I thought I wouldn't never see you again! Wherever have you been to?'

Bertie told her his adventure of the sea road into the west, and the sky ship, and the strange sailors that crewed it.

'At last they set me back in my own boat. How they found it and why they let me go, I can't say, as I can't say why they took me in the first place. You must be thinking as your Bertie has lost his wits and thinks he's been with the fairies. I promise you I be of sound mind and I bain't telling you no lie; but then I been asleep a time, so maybe it was just a dream. Tell me what you think, Alice. You don't believe as everything I told you can have happened, do you?'

Alice gave him a kiss and went to pick up something from the cupboard. She placed it in his hand. His knife, which he'd had many years, with his initials – 'A.A.', Albert Ashton – carved by his own hand in its haft.

When the visiting friar departed, he left the congregation of St Mary's with the conundrum of what to do with the anchor from the sky. Many of them were inclined to revere it as a holy relic. 'Why not compose a sermon about the symbolism of anchor and cross?' was the friar's parting shot to the priest. That was too vexing an assignment. The priest had a more practical bent. He had the blacksmith hammer the anchor into flat, curved pieces of metal to make ornate hinges for the church door.

Seven

St Arilda's Well

The time of Arthur was past, the Saxons were spreading inexorably west, yet in the civitas of the Dobunni, between the Severn's mouth and the headwaters of the Thames, Christian civilisation hung on. The Roman centuries had been a time of prosperity for the Dobunni as they farmed the rich land of the villas spaced between the three cities of Cirencester, Gloucester, and Bath. Though other British kingdoms to the north and east had fallen, the Dobunni remained sheltered behind their frontiers and tried to pretend the Roman Empire had never fallen.

In those days, a woman known to us as 'Arilda' came across the Severn from Gwent. She was the daughter of a high official at the royal court in Caerwent. She'd been married since her youth and had three sons now grown into men. Now in her forties, she'd agreed with her husband that their life together had run its course. They loved each other in a way, but they wanted no more children and both felt God's call upon the next part of their lives. So they went to the monastery: he to Caldey Island off the Dyfed coast, she to a tiny double monastery at Kington, near Oldbury, where the Romans used to operate a ferry across the Severn and the remains of a temple of Jupiter stood upon the hill.

The monastery was no more than a few thatched huts and a wooden church, and some cows and chickens, and gardens of vegetables and herbs, and fresh water from a spring. In this little fellowship of nuns and monks, surrounded by nature, Arilda spent her days in prayer and the sanctification of everyday tasks. It was a hard life compared with what she'd grown up with, but one in which she felt daily closer to God.

Meanwhile Ceawlin, King of the West Saxons, having defeated the British at Barbury and Bedford, looked west with covetous eyes to the fertile lands of the Dobunni. He knew their strength in arms was concentrated in the three cities. Bath was the smallest and located the greatest distance from the other two. So Ceawlin chose a point in the Dobunni's network of defences a few miles north of Bath: the fort on Hinton Hill, near Dyrham. His warbands used the cover of stream valleys to hide themselves from British scouts. By night they sneaked up Broadmead Brook, then swarmed over the hill fort's ramparts and by force of numbers overwhelmed its garrison.

Fleeing herdsmen took the news to Bath. King Fernfael sent riders to King Cynfael at Gloucester and King Cyndyddan at Cirencester. The three kings knew how often British kingdoms had been defeated one by one by a powerful invader. They knew they must fight the Roman way: they must combine their armies and apply maximum force at a single point. So Fernfael's men waited on the hills above Bath. Cyndyddan and Cynfael led their troops down the long miles to meet him. At the centre of the web, at Hinton Camp, Ceawlin's warriors felled trees and dug earth to strengthen the fort's defences.

In the fog of war, who can say exactly how it happened? Fernfael was there with his men, Cyndyddan with his, but Cynfael's army had a long march through forest and mire from Gloucester. They arrived late. They arrived tired. The Saxons were many. In the year 577, at Hinton Camp, Ceawlin fought the Dobunni and had victory. All three British kings were slain. Their cities were defenceless. The Saxons took them in quick succession and swarmed across the rich farmland, killing and pillaging as they pleased.

So it was that a Saxon thane called Muncius came with his warband to the little monastery at Kington. His eyes fell upon Arilda as she dug carrots from the earth. Her hands were soiled, her face was sweaty, she was far from young, yet she was handsome still and in her bearing was something of her high-born origin.

In barbarised Latin, Muncius said, 'Lead me to thy bed, woman.'

Her face turned white, she spoke no word, just carried on pulling carrots. You might expect that if he wanted her he'd have just taken her; it was a common enough thing at that time. But Muncius was proud. He was a strong warrior, tall and well made. He'd enjoyed many women and every one by their own consent. So he bided his time. He and his gang billeted themselves on the monastery and made the nuns and monks bring them bread and beer from their meagre supply.

Next morning, Muncius swaggered into the church when Arilda was praying alone.

'Come, woman! The day is fair and life is short. Let us swyve!'

With stiff dignity she rose from her knees. 'Do you not comprehend that this is a place consecrated by God?'

I daresay some of her words were too long for him to understand. 'The place matters not. We do it here or we do it outside in the trees. Either way is fine.'

'No!' she cried – and fled from the church.

When the warriors lounging in the sun saw Muncius appear at the church door and stare after the woman as she stamped away, they roared with beery laughter. Mighty Muncius spurned by a middle-aged nun! The thane's face darkened. The anger rose in him like a tide.

The next day, he followed her when she went to the spring to fetch water. By his warrior stealth he kept unseen. From the cover of the hazel bushes, he admired her freckled arms as she dipped the pails, and her silver-threaded auburn hair, and her serious mien. The reasons why she attracted him were maybe deeper than he understood. He knew only that he wanted her.

When he stepped out before her she let out a little cry. Her fingers darted to the wooden cross at her throat and she whispered a prayer to God.

'Let us play while the sun shines, my proud lady.'

'In God's name, no!'

With blatant repugnance she stared at him! He remembered how she'd humbled him before his men. The pulse of his lust throbbed in his ears.

'Your kings are dead!' he cried. 'You people, your lives and lands, are ours by right of war to do with what we please. I am a thane of the Hwicce. It is an honour I do thee. Lie with me and Woden will rejoice!'

'It is in the Lord God, King of Heaven, and his son Jesus Christ that I trust for my protection.'

Muncius saw the resolve in Arilda's eyes. 'So, let us test the strength of your God.'

He drew his sword and with one practised blow sliced off the woman's head. Her blood jetted into the pool and stained the water red.

The Saxon thane stalked back to the monastery. In cold fury he put the church to the torch. Then he led his warband to seek a place more hospitable to his needs and to scout out the best land on which to build his hall.

Arilda's brothers and sisters in the monastery mourned her brutal death; the people of Oldbury grieved her too. To honour her memory and her mortal remains, they agreed to build a new church. They began it on Shaw's Green in the centre of Oldbury, but they hadn't got far when an inundation from the Severn ruined what they'd done and they had to start again. Twice more the same thing happened. People said, 'God does not will that the church be built on this spot.' Others whispered, 'Nor does the Lady Sabrina.'

So they consulted an old hermit, who said, 'Take two white heifers that have never been milked, yoke them together, and set them free to wander. Where they stop to graze, that will be the place to build.'

The villagers did exactly as he said. The two heifers frisked straight out of the village and up the round hill where the pagan temple had stood, and began to crop the grass growing through the ruins. So it was on that sacred hilltop, on the temple's foundations, with a view across the Severn to the hills of Gwent where she was born, that they buried Arilda's body and built her church.

You might ask what meaning there can be in such an atrocity. You might ask where was the God in whom that woman placed her trust. Who can hope to answer such questions? Let me mention, though, one thing that some say: that although the Saxons conquered the Dobunni that fateful year of 577, though they reached the Severn and sundered for ever the Britons of Wales from the Britons of Dumnonia, the land of the Dobunni didn't cease to be a Christian land. There Saxon and Briton soon became one people, who spoke the Saxon tongue and followed the British faith. The civitas of the Dobunni became the kingdom of the Hwicce, which remained Christian even after it was annexed by pagan Mercia.

The spring where Arilda died became known as St Arilda's Well. It's a secluded, peaceful place, whose waters are said to have done many miracles of healing. Even today the waters have a reddish stain.

Eight

THE MOWER AND
THE BAILIFFS

It was haytime and Tom Smith was up at four in the morning to get on with mowing Farmer Gent's forty-acre meadow. He had to work as much as he could while the work was there, because he was behind in paying his rent to Farmer Flint. He kissed little Katie in her bed and the baby in the cot, got his bread and cider, and his scythe from the shed, called goodbye to Mary who'd gone to feed the pig, and as he came back round the cottage he heard a fizzing from the bee skep in the corner of the yard and knew those bees were about ready to swarm. It was that time of year when everything seethes with life. Got to make hay while the sun shines. He was doing that all right.

Jack Pearce was waiting in the lane with his scythe. They made their way between the new fences and hedges down to the meadow. It was to pay for the fencing of his allocation that Farmer Flint had increased the rent. The 'improvement' of the land would benefit us all, he'd said. It might benefit him. All it meant for Tom was more rent to pay and more work to be done for other men. He used to have his own strips in the big fields, and his own cows and sheep on the commons, before the Parliamentary Enclosure came to these lush pastures between Chipping Sodbury and Pucklechurch. Now he was just a day labourer for those who owned the land.

The sun was already driving off the morning mist when they reached Farmer Gent's meadow, which Tom had given preference to over his landlord's own meadow because Farmer Gent paid better. Soon the rhythmic swish of their scythes, like a song and dance, was slicing through the grass and clover, the buttercups and fairy flax. It was a shame to see all those flowers fall, but they'd soon be going over anyway and they'd make tasty fodder for the cattle come winter. As the long morning wore on, the sun rose higher till it was beating down fierce and hot and the sweat was running down the men's backs as they toiled.

'Time to rest,' said Jack at last.

Under the shade of a hedgerow elm they sat to take their bread and cider. As it was so nation hot, they rested there a while afterwards and smoked their pipes, till Tom saw the dark clouds massing in the distance and felt a sticky charge in the air.

'Weather a-coming. Best be getting on whilst we can. The sooner this meadow be done, the more sooner we can mow another.'

They whetted their scythes and got back to work, but they hadn't been mowing long when a figure appeared at the gate across the meadow. It was a woman with a baby, hard to make out at such a distance, but as she hurried towards them Tom saw it was his own sweet Mary. Must be something amiss for her to come all this way. She'd come out without her bonnet, and her hair was half undone, her face wet with tears, and when she reached him she was sobbing so much she couldn't speak.

'What be a-nagging thee, Mary?'

'I don't know what we'll do!' she wept.

Tom jumped at the worst it might be. 'Has something happened to Katie?'

'No, it bain't that. O Tom!'

'Has the pig died?'

'No, not that.'

Tom took her close in his arms. 'Tell I, poppet, what's come to pass?'

'It be Farmer Flint – he a-sent the bums to take possession against the rent as be owing. They be making a list of everything we have, from the bedstead to the last teaspoon, the pig and chickens and all, to put the lot to auction.'

Tom swore a foul curse. 'The wuzberd could a-waited till I'd earned enough to pay his blasted rent.'

'But what shall we do?'

'Get thee back to the house, Mary, and take the children to thy mother's. I'll come back in a little while and sort out they bailies.'

'O Tom, thee won't be violent, will 'ee?' Thee won't kill them? They'd hang 'ee for sure and I and the children shall be paupers in the workhouse.'

'I won't touch them, I promise. Away with thee now and I'll see thee at thy mother's' – and off she went with the babe to do as he said.

'Should 'ee not be a-wending?' asked Jack.

'Time enough for that. Let's mow another acre whilst the sun yet be a-shining.'

They plied their scythes for another hour, till one more acre was cut into flowery swathes of hay. The air was still close, the storm not yet come, when Tom got home. The cottage was oddly silent. Even the hens in the yard and the pig in the sty made no sound. He hid his scythe in the hedge – what would he do if they took that? – and went inside, where three bailiffs were sitting in his chairs and peacefully smoking their pipes as if it were a public house.

'How be you, gentlemen?' said Tom, very polite. 'What brings you hither?'

'You know well enough, Tom Smith,' said one. 'Your rent be in arrears by six pound eighteen bob and sixpence as was due last Lady Day. We have taken possession on Mr Flint's orders and made an inventory of what you have.'

'I see. And may I ask how long you'll be abiding in possession?'

'Till the debt be paid, or auction day, whichever comes the sooner.'

'You've put everything on the list, have you?'

'We have indeed.'

'There may be one thing as you won't have put down.'

'What would that be?'

'I'll fetch him and you can see if you has to include him.'

Tom moseyed out to the secluded corner of the yard where the bee skep was excitedly buzzing. In the hole in the top he could see the fluttering of wings and the darting of keen little faces. Ever so carefully he wrapped a piece of sackcloth over the skep, then lifted the whole thing on the plank on which it stood, and carried it indoors.

'What is it then?' said one of the bailiffs, list and pen at the ready.

'Take a look if thee wilt.'

The three bum-bailiffs eyed the veiled shape. One reached for the sackcloth.

Another said, 'What's that buzzing noise?'

Too late. The man had pulled the sacking away. As Tom slipped out the door and closed it behind him, the bees boiled from the hive in a frenzy. Safe behind the hedge, Tom listened to the manly screams of pain resounding in the cottage. The door flung open. The three bums ran out, cleared the fence, and fled across the field, sprinting for all they were worth, with the swarm of angry bees in hot pursuit.

Tom went back to fetch the skep out to its place in the yard. He secured all the windows, collected Mary's box of rings, locked the door, pocketed the key, and made his way over the hill to his mother-in-law's.

Mary came rushing out to meet him. 'Tell I, Tom, hast thee killed them? Shalt thee be hanged?'

Tom laughed, and kissed her, and told her what had happened. Mary was mollified a bit, she even laughed, but she knew it wasn't the end of the matter, as the debt was still unpaid. Tom left her to her worrying and repaired to Farmer Gent's fine old farmhouse to inform him how many acres had been mowed.

'What's this I hear,' said Farmer Gent, 'of three fellows hollering through yonder fields with a swarm of bees after them?'

So Tom told him too the tale of the bailiffs' misfortune.

Farmer Gent laughed loud and long. 'You know why Mr Flint is pressing you so hard for that rent? It's because he's irked you've given preference to my meadow over his.' And there and then he wrote a cheque to cover the amount Tom owed.

Tom was not too proud to thank him kindly and take the money to pay off his arrears. It was a nice piece of charity and brings this tale to a cheerful end, but Tom knew well enough that, the way things now were, there were owners and there were labourers and that he was indebted just as much to Farmer Gent as he'd been to Farmer Flint, only in a different kind of way.

Nine

THE DISCOVERY
OF AMERICA

Sailors in the North Atlantic had long known about the islands
in the west. There was the Island of Brasil, a paradise on earth
beyond the sea mist, one and the same perhaps as the Land of
Promise to which St Brendan came in his coracle. There was the
Island of Seven Cities, named after the cities founded by the seven
bishops of a boatload of refugees fleeing Spain after the Moorish
conquest, and sometimes called 'Antillia' as if to suggest it lay
before the coast of another land beyond. The fishermen of Bristol
knew these stories. When they sailed up to Iceland they heard
something too of lands beyond Greenland which the Norsemen
had visited: of Helluland, Markland, and Vinland the Good.

Bristol's trade in cod from Iceland was harassed by the long
reach of the Hanseatic League, which demanded the exclusion
of all but the Hanseatic ports from Icelandic trade. So the Bristol
men voyaged further west across the grey Atlantic, to new waters
teeming with cod. But if you caught fish so far away, there was a
risk they'd rot before you got them home. The answer was to salt
and dry them. For that you needed dry land nearby on which to
set out wooden stages. There was good money to be made, thanks

to England's inexhaustible demand for cod, so by 1480 ships were sailing from Bristol every year in search of the Island of Brasil, some of them carrying salt, and it wasn't long before fishing boats were coming into Bristol with cargoes of cod ready-salted and dried. The Bristol seamen were canny; they kept shtum about where all this salted cod was coming from.

But Bristol ships had business elsewhere too. One time, one such ship was moored in the Spanish port of Huelva to take on gunpowder and oranges. Some of the crew knew the place well. They knew the taverns. They knew the women. One night the Andalusian wine made one sailor's tongue wag too freely. He boasted to some greenhorns how far he'd voyaged – 'I tell you, we trod the shore of the Island of Brasil.' One of the serving wenches, who'd learnt a little English, overheard him. Word passed from her – don't ask me how – to a friar of the monastery across the estuary, and so to its prior, Antonio de Marchena.

It so happened that a frequent visitor to Huelva, and a friend of Marchena, was a Genoese dreamer by the name of Christopher Columbus – a man who believed that God had granted his life a special purpose, who yearned for St Brendan's paradise across the sea, who believed that by sailing west you could reach the fabulous lands of the East and somewhere near them God's own paradise on earth. The mathematicians said it was too far, that if you sailed for China you'd never make it home. But 'The English have found Brasil,' Marchena told Columbus. There really was land in the west near enough to reach in a well-rigged ship. So Columbus sought backing from the King of Portugal. 'A direct route I promise you to the spices, jewels and gold of the East.' He tried the King of England too. They both turned him down. It was under the banners of Castile and Aragon that Columbus crossed the ocean blue in 1492 and discovered land exactly where he expected: islands that he believed lay close to the Asian shore.

He returned in triumph and processed through Spain with a grand entourage to the royal court in Barcelona. The route passed through Valencia. At his reception in that city Columbus met a fellow Genoese, his name John Cabot, who was supervising the construction of a new harbour and was very experienced in maritime trade. Cabot had visited the entrepôts in the Levant where the spice caravans arrived from the East. Shrewdly, he studied the spices, plants and skins Columbus had brought from his 'Indies', and the naked 'Indians' who excited his admiring audiences. Cabot saw that none of these resembled the produce and people of the East he'd seen with his own eyes.

He said to Columbus, 'The distance you've sailed seems much less than the Mohammedan mathematicians have calculated as the distance to reach China.'

'They exaggerate! Christian scholars have long known the earth cannot be so large.'

'You put faith in theology over mathematics?'

'And have I not been proved right?'

Yet Cabot saw a gleam in Columbus's eye and knew there was something more that the man had known to make him so certain that land could be found. What else could that be but solid information that some ship had at last found Brasil or the Seven Cities? Cabot knew the mathematicians were right, that Columbus couldn't have got anywhere near China. There had to be a better route northwards, where the earth's curvature would reduce the distance. Surely that was where Brasil lay. The rewards of finding such a route, and bypassing the Turkish middlemen, would be incalculable. So Cabot took his own scheme for a voyage of exploration to the monarchs of Portugal and Spain. When they turned him down, he went to the only place left to try: to England.

In the Italian community in London he found an ally in one Giovanni Antonio Carbonaro of the Hermit Friars of St Augustine, who saw in Cabot's plans a chance to take the word of God to new lands, new peoples, even all the way to China. Thanks to this friar, Cabot was granted an audience with King Henry VII.

'What interest can there be for England where Spain has already claimed the sea road to the East?' asked the King, who surely lamented that he'd let Columbus slip between his fingers.

'I assure Your Majesty that Columbus has not reached the vicinity of China as he believes. China is thousands of miles beyond. All he has found are islands in the middle of a vast ocean.'

'If that be so, how do you propose to accomplish what Columbus has not?'

'By sailing north-west, via the Island of Brasil, in whose location I believe Your Majesty's subjects have a certain interest.'

The King looked back at Cabot with an inscrutable gaze.

'In northern latitudes,' continued Cabot, 'it will be a relatively short distance to the extremities of Asia, from which one may then simply follow the coast to China.'

'So bypassing the new Spanish colonies in the tropics.' The King smiled a cunning smile. 'We like your plan, Cabot. But please understand the sensitivity we must exercise towards our Spanish friends. We shall grant you a patent to voyage north, west, east, to claim in England's name whatever lands you discover, but forbidding you to go south where the Spaniards sail.'

So John Cabot came to Bristol, where he rented a house in St Nicholas Street and his interests were entrusted to the King's representative: Richard Ameryk, Customs Collector. Well did Cabot need Ameryk's help. The Bristol merchants were wary of this Genoese interloper. It wasn't many years since Genoese vessels had ambushed an expedition of Bristol merchantmen that had tried to breach the Italian monopoly on Mediterranean trade; and they were anxious above all to keep their new cod fisheries from foreign attention.

The only financial backing Cabot could raise was from the Italian merchants in London, so it was in one small caravel, named *Matthew* after his wife Mattea, with a crew of eighteen that he braved the Atlantic in 1496. By English maritime law in those days, the crew's vote held sway over important decisions at sea. It took no more than a storm and a few close encounters with icebergs for Cabot's crew to decide, against his wishes, to turn back.

With Ameryk's help, Cabot recruited a more stalwart crew and in 1497 the *Matthew* made a second foray into the ocean. But his Bristol seamen had little interest in reaching China.

All they really cared about was cod. They didn't want a foreign navigator to know the secret location where the cod were salted and dried, so they fiddled with the course he was trying to steer and the *Matthew* sailed further south than Cabot had intended, where the ocean is wider, beating into the wind all the way.

By the grace of God, on 24 June, St John the Baptist's Day, they made landfall on a wild wooded shore. The sky was clear, the sun was hot, and the land well watered. His heart pounding with joy, Cabot gave thanks to God, erected a cross, and planted the banners of the King of England, the Pope, and St Mark of Venice. The land seemed strangely still. The only sounds were the waves, the crickets, the calling of birds, yet the seamen had the feeling of being watched by unseen eyes. They never left sight of the ship, as they were few in number and dared not risk ambush in this new land so far from home. If they saw no people, they saw evidence of them: snares, a carved stick, a fireplace, felled trees, and a track heading inland. Surely the natives were there, watching them.

Soon enough, the *Matthew* took on water from a stream and set sail, coasting north-east, heading for home. Now they'd discovered land, the important thing was to report it. Cabot called it the 'Island of St John', but as he sailed along the coast, unbroken for hundreds of miles, it became clear this was no minor island. He was convinced it was a long arm of the Asian mainland extending far to the north and east of China. It was wild and wooded all the way. Just once they glimpsed running figures – whether human or animal they couldn't tell.

At last the coast turned sharply north-west and they were into the open sea. It was a speedy crossing with the wind behind them, but once again the crew, still obsessing about the cod fisheries, obfuscated Cabot's navigation and the *Matthew* made land too far south, in Brittany, and had to sail back around Land's End to reach Bristol.

So John Cabot returned to England in triumph, like Columbus in Spain four years previously. King Henry gladly granted him an audience. He knew a good thing when he saw it.

'I have found the mainland,' said Cabot. 'Give me ships and

crews and I will follow its coast to China, and England shall have a sea route to all the treasures of the East.'

The King furnished him with a ship. Brother Carbonaro and the Italian friars stumped up for a second. Even the Bristol merchants now saw the promise in Cabot's enterprise. There was money to be made, and the virgin seas along these new shores would surely be teeming with cod. They clubbed together to fund three further ships.

When Cabot returned to Bristol from London his success had gone to his head. He came dressed in fine silks and dispensed magnanimous gestures to everyone he loved. To the friars he promised bishoprics in the new lands. To his barber he promised an island as his personal estate. When Richard Ameryk brought word the King had granted him a pension, Cabot was so moved with gratitude that he said, 'In honour of all you have done to support my cause I shall name after you the mainland territory I have discovered. I shall call it "Ameryka".'

In 1498, with his fleet of five vessels, provisioned for a year, Cabot sailed west a third time. They hadn't got far when the ships were scattered to the four winds by one of the Atlantic's great storms. Into the western mists those five ships made their separate ways. A year went by and not one of them had returned. They were given up for lost and never seen again … or so the story was told.

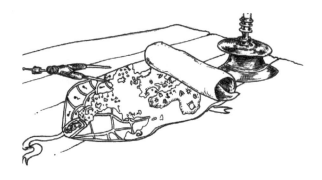

But it's not quite the end of the story. For the Spaniards and Italians have their own stories, hidden in archives and bank vaults, from which one may piece together what happened.

Finding his flagship alone, Cabot knew there was little hope of meeting its sister ships in the ocean's vastness. The best course was to continue to his new-discovered coast – which Spain's spies reported to Columbus was none other than the Island of the Seven Cities and which is today called Nova Scotia. With that one ship Cabot pressed on with his plan, coasting west and south, to seek the great cities of the East. Yet for mile after mile, for thousands of miles, the land remained wilderness, its people mere hunters and fishers living in small villages. Gradually the coast trended more southward than westward, and still no sign of cities or civilisation, until at last the truth was forced upon Cabot that this land he was charting was no part of Asia: it was some other continent that stood in the way.

They reached a southern cape where the coastline turned north. In the miasmic air of this torrid clime many of the crew, Cabot included, fell victim to a debilitating fever. It was hard to think, hard to work the ship. Cabot was torn between the hope it might yet be possible to find a way through to Asia and the impulse to head home. Through a tropical archipelago, peopled by naked natives like those Columbus had brought to Spain, they sailed south, till they reached a jungle coast trending east–west. Cabot had charted new lands on a scale beyond what any other navigator in Europe had accomplished. He knew it was time to go home. He gave the order to coast eastwards.

By now the English ship was deep inside the region where the Spaniards were establishing colonies. What Cabot didn't know was that a Spanish expedition was charting this same coast – of what today is Venezuela – from the opposite direction. It was commanded by a cut-throat adventurer by the name of Alonso de Ojeda. Off the Coquibaçoa peninsula, Ojeda's fleet encountered the stray English vessel. There was no contest. Outgunned, outnumbered, her crew crippled by fever, the English ship was boarded.

Cabot watched helplessly as Ojeda and his lieutenants ransacked his cabin and unrolled the great map on which he'd charted all the coasts he'd discovered. Some say that Ojeda, in ruthless prosecution of Spain's interests, slaughtered Cabot and his men and threw their bodies to the sharks. Others say he only confiscated their charts and ordered the ship out of Spanish waters ... and so Cabot's flagship was able to limp north to reach at last the Island of Brasil, soon to become 'Newfoundland', where he found that Carbonaro and his friars had built a wooden church to minister to the crews of the other Bristol ships, who in Cabot's absence had been busy fishing for cod.

A year overdue, Cabot returned to Bristol. His health was broken by fever and, though not yet fifty, he died a few months later. His fame was already being overtaken by history. Among those with Ojeda scrutinising the map in Cabot's cabin was a young Florentine banker called Amerigo Vespucci. As Vespucci's eye followed the outline of the large northern continent Cabot had discovered, he couldn't help noticing the name inscribed in large letters upon it: 'Ameryka'. Nor could he help noticing the similarity of that name to his own Christian name, Amerigo. Perhaps it was then that the seeds were sown of Vespucci's ambition to rewrite the history of the New World so that he – and not Columbus or Cabot or the native people who'd been there thousands of years – should be recognised as its discoverer and that it should be named after him: as 'America'.

Ten

BETTY'S GRAVE

When Betty was a young woman in Poulton she was in love with a man called Hugh. He liked her in a way, but she was half Gypsy and he thought himself a bit of a gent and reckoned he could net a woman of higher station.

'I'm sorry,' he told Betty. 'The truth is I just don't find you very comely.'

How can you argue with that? Betty looked in the mirror and saw that she was plain. She went to the hedge witch, who gave her potions, but they didn't seem to work. Hugh barely deigned to notice her when they passed in the street.

Poor Betty had lost her heart to him. One evening she tramped off through the fields. Her heart was aching, the tears were running down her face, and she didn't know what to do. When she came to the wood, she walked on through the may blossom and thigh-deep froth of cow parsley, all lit by the golden evening light, the whole wood full of loveliness that mocked her broken heart. She heard a trickling of water, and in the shade of a great twisted willow, hedged with brambles and briars, she found a pool in which she saw her features reflected thin and wan.

'How I wish I had the power to win what I desire!'

And from beneath the briars appeared a snake.

'You can have power to win your desire,' it hissed, 'if seven nights in a row you bathe here in my pool.'

Betty was entranced by the promise of those words. She took off her clothes and, wincing as thorns scraped her skin, she eased into the chilly pool beside the serpent and baptised her body beneath the rising moon. The next six nights she returned to bathe again with the snake. On the seventh night, as she walked home she could feel in herself the power to win her desire. In the mirror, next morning, she saw that she was beautiful. When she went to get some milk, there was a swing in her hips and all the men she passed turned their heads to look.

But that very morning, as luck had it, her beloved Hugh was married to a bonny lass from a good family in Oxfordshire, and departed with his bride to Portsmouth, where they boarded a boat to carry them overseas.

Betty had no need to grieve for long. There were plenty of other fellows to come courting a woman so beautiful. It was one called Jonah she married – a small-time farmer from Fairford, a humble fellow, not proud like Hugh. He couldn't believe his luck to have won a wife so fine, whose Gypsy charms made the other women green with envy and the other men jealous she wasn't theirs. She loved him with all her heart, as he loved her with all of his. You might think that would make a happy ending. But Betty's bargain with the snake brought her power to win desires beyond mere beauty of face and form. In the midst of his slumbers, Jonah noticed that sometimes Betty would rise from the bed at midnight and vanish from the room. As any man might who's blessed with a ravishing wife, he wondered where she went.

One night he kept awake, feigning sleep, till Betty began to rise. Up in a flash, he caught her wrist tight.

'Let me go!'

'I will, my sweet, so long as you take me with you wherever you be wending to.'

She looked at him uncertainly. 'All right, you may come, but you must take care to speak no word till we're back safe and sound in bed.'

Jonah followed her downstairs and to his astonishment saw his wife, nightgown and all, funnel out through the keyhole of the door; and then by the power of her will she sucked him through the keyhole after her. Waiting in the moonlight were two milk-white calves. Betty leapt astride one, Jonah the other, and side by side they galloped almost flying across the landscape of the night. Hedges, ditches, brambles – easily the calves hurdled them. Jonah's heart leapt with the thrill. Betty smiled at him from her steed. When they reached the Thames the calves didn't slow down. With a tremendous leap they cleared its width – they were still sailing through the air when Jonah, too amazed to stop himself, cried out, 'That be a good jump for a calf!'

The instant the words left his lips the calf's back shot from beneath him and he was pitched with a splash into the shallows near the bank – while Betty and the calves raced on. But truly

Betty loved her husband. Before the night was done she came jockeying back to collect him. Many times afterwards they rode together those milk-white calves, and Jonah remembered not to break the night's enchantment with words. And that wasn't all. Betty took him to swim like trout beneath the Coln's clear waters and to scramble like squirrels in the treetops of Lea Wood. She made them as small as rabbits, led by a glow-worm to light the way, while they snooped inside the warren on Marston Hill.

Then Jonah got ill. It was one of those things that happen, no rhyme or reason to blame. And Betty's power to win her desire held no power over her husband's disease. She gathered herbs from the fields, she brewed potions like a hedge witch, but it did no good; her beloved Jonah slipped away from her and died.

People cope in different ways when their loved one dies. Betty couldn't cope at all. She'd loved Jonah with all her heart, as he'd loved her with all of his. Now her heart was broken. Her mind became unhinged. She thought he'd left her, rejected her, like Hugh. In dead of night she sought the way to the snake's pool to beg the power to get back her desire. But the woods were deep, the brooks were many, and the brambles and briars were fierce and thick.

One morning in Poulton they found her wandering naked in the street. Her flesh was cut by thorns, her hair a tangle of knots and burrs; she couldn't speak sense to say why she was there. There were some who didn't recognise her. There were many who did, women who'd envied her, men who'd fancied her, all now disgusted by her ageing abject body. One kindly old couple sheltered her in their cottage. But their kindness could not heal Betty's broken heart, or her madness. On moonlit nights she sought in vain the serpent's pool, she gathered herbs from the wayside, hoping to win her beloved Hugh, to save her beloved Jonah.

'Her be a strange one all right,' they said, and feared her because of her strangeness and because she was half Gypsy. When a ewe or cow gave birth to stillborn young they said, 'It must be Betty as put a curse on she.' When a gate fell off its hinges they said it was Betty who'd done it. When the pump broke down and they couldn't get water, well, Betty must have cursed the pump. When the cream in the buttery wouldn't set she must have cursed the cream. And when a child fell sick, 'It be Betty as a-witchified him.'

So the wicked words spread; a way to make sense of misfortune, a way to point the finger of blame away from the guilty secrets inside your own soul. One thing led to another, hatred became hysteria, and when the sick boy died they screamed, 'It do be Betty's work, that evil witch!' and quoted the Good Book: 'Thee shalt not suffer a witch to live.'

The angry mob dragged her to the crossroads half a mile out of Poulton. A crossroads, so her ghost wouldn't know which road to take. By that crossroads they hanged her and buried her. But the power of Betty's will was strong. Two mornings later in Poulton they found her in the street again, naked, thorn-scratched, mumbling about 'the serpent's pool'. They didn't think; they only did. They dragged her back to the crossroads and hanged her and buried her a second time. Yet still the grave couldn't hold her grief. Not two days later she was back in Poulton in the same state as before. When they took her to the gallows again, she said, 'If you want me to stay quiet in my grave, then you best show some respect while I'm dead and keep it nicely decked with flowers.'

They never thought of mercy. They hanged her and buried her a third time, but they remembered what she'd said and the women adorned the grave with flowers. After that there was no sign of poor Betty. They laid flowers for her every spring and she lay quiet beneath the sod as the long years went by. Till things started to get modern and incomers came and people began to forget the old ways. By the 1970s everything had got so supersonic that flowers no longer placed on Betty's grave. Her sad ghost stirred again; she stalked the streets of Fairford in search of her lost husband, and frightened old women late at night by begging them for healing herbs. So the custom of laying flowers on the grave resumed and Betty's ghost returned to its sleep.

Yet even today people will look for something to blame for their misfortune. Things untoward and annoying in that neighbourhood still get blamed on Betty's unquiet soul. When lately I've passed by the crossroads, I've seen no sign of flowers laid on Betty's grave.

Eleven

THE FLYING PEAR TREES

On the road out from Newent towards Gloucester you may notice in the hedgerow five splendid pear trees. Easy to confuse with the cherry trees nearby, but there they are, five pear trees, and I mean proper domestic pear trees, *Pyrus communis*, not wild ones, and lovely tasty pears they have too. You might think that's odd to find them in the hedgerow instead of an orchard. And you'd be right, because originally those trees *were* in an orchard, miles away in the Vale of Evesham. Well, it wasn't exactly an orchard, more just a corner of a meadow. The farmer who owned them picked the fruit every September and he really loved those pears – so juicy and tasty and just the right balance between crisp and soft so long as you picked them at the right time.

Only thing was, the rooks that roosted in the spinney beside the meadow knew exactly when the right time was. Top cock of them was a strange fellow – completely white, so you'd think he was an albino, except his eyes weren't pink, but black like any other rook's. You might think he'd get persecuted, but no, he was the boss; he had a slinky shiny black mate and you could tell his progeny by the little patches of white on their wings. This clever white rook would watch the pears each day. When he saw a blush of pink on their skin, he knew they were ready. He croaked the word, and down the rooks came, hundreds of them, like a flurry of black rags on the wind, to peck with gusto at the fruit.

When the farmer came rushing out, yelling and gesticulating, the rooks paid not a blind bit of notice. They knew he couldn't harm them without his gun. By the time he'd fetched it, the rooks had had their feast. With a mocking glance from his beady black eyes the white rook would give the signal and away they'd fly, wheeling into the sky on swift strong beats of their wings. The farmer would fire a couple of shots after them, but the damage was already done. All that was left swinging by their stalks on the branches were ragged pecked cores.

One year the farmer got so furious that he had an idea. 'That be the last time they rascals do scrump my pears!' All through the year that followed, he brooded on his plan, watching the rooks as they cawed in the spinney; watching as the flock gyred in the sky each dusk like some vast elemental phantom; watching especially that cheeky white cock who thought he was God's gift to the Vale.

September came round again and the pears were swelling on the branches. The rooks were watching them, waiting. The farmer was watching the pears too, waiting for the first hint of pink. At last he saw it. One more day and the pears would be ready. That evening, when the rooks had settled in their roosts, the farmer mixed nut oil with fermented holly bark to make a bucketful of birdlime, then he took a ladder to each of the pear trees in turn and painted the birdlime on the branches, all around the pear stalks.

In the morning he waited by the farmhouse window. In the September sun the pears had an appetising blush of pink. The white rook cawed in anticipation, and stretched his wings, and down he flew. The rest of the mob came soaring after him. They were so eager to feast that they didn't notice the birdlime into which their feet sank. They just set to at the pears with their big grey beaks.

As they feasted, the birdlime hardened in the hot sun. It took them a while to notice, so intent were they on eating. Then one bird let out a squawk as she discovered her feet were stuck fast. One after another, in quick succession, they all discovered the same thing. They flapped their wings and cawed their consternation, but they couldn't get free.

When the farmer heard the racket, he picked up his gun and ambled out to the meadow. No need to hurry. There they were, those feathered thieves, stuck helpless in the trees. That cheeky white one as helpless as the rest. He'd be the first for a barrelful of shot.

The white rook saw the farmer lift his gun. He croaked a loud rattling cry and beat his wings with all his strength. The others did the same. They flapped as hard as they could to try to pull their feet free. In that kaleidoscope of flapping black wings, the farmer didn't know where to aim. And then, with common cause, the rooks started to beat their wings in time with each other. Such terrific force that something had to yield. From where the trees were rooted came a straining and a creaking, the rooks flapped yet harder, and with a slithering, creaking, groaning the roots of the trees pulled free of the ground. The farmer's jaw dropped wide as he saw his five pear trees borne aloft

on the rooks' beating wings and away through the sky, trunks dangling, roots swinging in the wind.

South-west they flew, across the wide meanders of the Avon, over the whaleback of Bredon Hill. Folk working in the fields near Tewkesbury gazed up with open mouths at the pear trees flying by, their branches fringed by hundreds of flapping black wings. Across the Severn they went, towards May Hill and the wooded hills of Dean.

But now the sky was dark with grey clouds. Soon it began to rain. The raindrops soaked into the birdlime holding the rooks' feet to the branches. The birdlime began to wash away. All of a sudden, all at once, the birds' toes came free. The rooks lurched upwards on the force of their wingbeats. The pear trees plummeted down, and down, and down, and landed – thunk, thunk, thunk, thunk, thunk – in the hedgerow beside that road out of Newent.

I guess the trees didn't suffer too badly for their airborne adventure, as their roots quickly found purchase in their new location, and the trees continued to flourish, and to produce each September a fine crop of pears, juicy and delicious, ripe to be picked or pecked by any passing walker or bird. There they remain to this day if you look hard enough to find them.

Twelve

THE SECRET OF THE GAUNTS' CHAPEL

King Henry VII enjoyed his stays at the manor of Acton Court, whose peaceful gardens and fields were much preferable to the noisy smelly city of Bristol, where on occasion he had business with the merchants. Sir Robert Poyntz had reason to be hospitable, having been knighted by Henry after the Battle of Bosworth Field that won him the Crown, but the King's visit was quite an imposition, with his train of many courtiers, servants and soldiers.

In this entourage was a young courtier called John Coleman. Amidst the hustle and bustle, no one noticed how this young man caught the eye of Sir Robert's raven-haired young daughter, Mary. Discreetly they slipped away to walk together among the tall clipped hedges. John was not yet twenty, Mary a few years younger. In just two days they'd fallen in love. In a shadowy green lane between two yew hedges, they held hands and gazed in each other's eyes and pledged their undying love.

Unfortunately they were not as alone as they'd thought. Sir Robert had noticed his daughter's absence and learnt from a gardener that she'd headed to this secluded part of the grounds.

From behind the hedge he heard their fevered words and their vigorous teenage kissing. Out he leapt, furious as the Devil.

'Keep away from my daughter, you villain, or you'll feel for sure the weight of the clenched fist!'

By 'clenched fist' he referred to the Poyntz rebus: 'poign' being a pun on the family name. From the look on Sir Robert's face John could believe he meant the threat more literally.

'As for you, my young trollop, away with you to your room! Let's see if a diet of bread and water won't cool your blood!'

In tears and anguish Mary fled to the house. Sobbing in her room, she pulled from her hair – what her father hadn't seen – the gold bodkin John had slotted there as a token of his eternal love. She trusted his pledge with all her heart, that he'd find a way to come for her. All she had to do was wait.

Meanwhile, Sir Robert complained to the King: 'With the greatest respect, sire, it is a trespass to our hospitality that one of Your Majesty's young fellows should make advances to my daughter of such tender years.'

Cunning King Henry valued Sir Robert's friendship. He dismissed John Coleman at once from his service and sent him packing back to London.

John loved Mary Poyntz with all his heart, but he hadn't a hope of marrying her unless he first distinguished himself in some way. He had neither money nor rank. He was no warrior. He decided his best bet was to become a scholar, so thereby to become of use to the King and be taken back into his service.

To Padua he went. He studied with all the vigour of his yearning to make himself worthy of Mary. He heard no word from her, but he trusted her, that she would be faithful to their pledge. He didn't dare write, for fear her father would intercept the letters.

Skill in scholarship, the learning of languages, takes time. The years pass by quicker than you ever expect they will. John was a man past thirty when at last his friends at court secured from the new king, Henry VIII, his appointment to a diplomatic post in which his linguistic skills could be put to use in reaping intelligence for the Crown.

John's heart soared with the dream that at last seemed in reach. He risked a letter to Mary, via a friend of a friend, telling her about his appointment, declaring his undiminished love, hoping they might soon consummate their love before God.

In Calais, awaiting the ship to England, he met an acquaintance of his youth who had connections in Gloucestershire. Pretending a nonchalance he did not feel, he asked the man, 'What news of the Poyntzes of Iron Acton?'

'Old Sir Robert soldiers on. Has a place in the Queen's household.'

'And his children?'

'Married and breeding, most of them.'

John fought to keep the tremor from his voice. 'And Mary too?'

'Not married yet, despite her years' – John half let go a sigh of relief – 'but a rich old gentleman from outside the county has lately made an offer, and she has accepted him.'

There was more to the story of Mary's engagement than John's informant knew. All these years she had avoided any entanglement. Her heart had been loyal to John. But when this latest offer came she was nigh on thirty and her father, perceiving the advantage of the alliance, insisted she accept – on pain of being shut away in a nunnery. She resisted as long as she could, till not only was she convinced her father would carry out his threat, but a friend in whom she'd confided said, 'Open your eyes to the truth. If your sweetheart hasn't come for you by now, has never even written, you can be sure he'll have forgotten all about you by now and be married to a wench more fitting to his rank.'

Reluctantly Mary yielded to her aged suitor's proposal. But then, only days before John reached Calais, John's letter arrived, delayed by its circuitous route. At once all her feelings were awoken. She remembered that day between the yew hedges, his lips on hers, his hands on her waist. She felt a churning in her loins, such as she'd never before known, all the stronger because her natural instincts had been held in check so many years. She could not marry the man she was betrothed to. Better to go to the nunnery than marry anyone but her beloved John.

It never came to that. Her father died. Her brother Sir Anthony, who inherited his estate, wanted her to be happy, and his wife Lady Jane was her good friend. Mary was free to break her engagement. On tenterhooks she waited at Acton Court for John Coleman to come.

John knew none of this; only that Mary had accepted another. He never boarded the ship from Calais. His hopes and dreams were shattered. England held nothing for him except the memory of the love he'd lost. He didn't know where to go, except away from England. Fate took him to the Rhine, where he found refuge in a monastery in which his scholarly skills were appreciated. He could not think of finding love with any other woman. Better to devote his unspent passion to God. He became a monk, and a priest. He passed his days in study and prayer. He tried not

to think of Mary. The years passed, like a stream running quick beneath a bridge, and John cared not; the passing of the years of his life could only bring him closer to his destiny in God.

Then one day the monastery had a visitor, an Englishman returning from Rome. His name was John Essex and he was the Abbot of St Augustine's in Bristol. Just to hear mention of Bristol, a place so close to Acton Court, made John Coleman tremble inside. He wanted to ask after Mary Poyntz, as he'd done in Calais long years before, but he was now a man of God; it would be a peril to his soul even to speak her name. The Abbot was a shrewd man and might have divined the true import of such a question. As it was, he was impressed by John's abilities and perceived in his conversation a longing for England, and Gloucestershire especially.

'Listen, Coleman, the mastership of the Gaunts' Hospital is vacant and falls under my jurisdiction. If you'd like the job, it's yours.'

The Gaunts' Hospital was a priory adjacent to St Augustine's Abbey with a mission to feed the poor. I daresay Bristol's proximity to Acton Court was one reason John accepted that invitation, but upon arriving in the city he was determined to discipline his soul and made no attempt to contact Mary, whom he presumed to be married and perhaps dwelling far from Iron Acton.

Spiritual peril turned out to be closer than John expected. Before he died, Sir Robert Poyntz had paid for a splendid fan-vaulted chantry chapel to be added to the hospital's church. There he was buried and there members of his family often came to pray. Moreover, as the house now had only four resident brothers, there was space for a few lay gentlefolk to stay as boarders, of whom one was Lady Jane, the widow of Mary's brother.

One day, as John passed Jane's quarters, he saw her welcoming a guest – a woman slender in build, dressed in black like a widow, with raven hair threaded with grey. It was just a glimpse before the two women vanished behind the door, but John's heart began to thud in response to something about that black figure, something perhaps in the motion of the shoulders as they turned.

He told himself it was his imagination. He made himself attend to his duties and devotions. But the very next day, in the Poyntz chapel, when he thought he'd finished the queue of penitents he'd been confessing, he saw one last figure waiting at the entrance. The woman in black. For a moment the image of the girl he'd carried in his memory was superimposed on that of the middle-aged woman before him, her face gaunt and pale, the bloom of youth spent. Yet she was beautiful to him and he loved her as much as he always had. In the cover of his alcove he gave no sign that he knew her. He lowered his eyes from the alabaster curve of her cheek and, as the blood thudded in his temple, he listened to her confession.

'Father, I have sinned, if sin it be. Since my youth, I have been consumed with love for a man I met then. For years I hoped and prayed he would come to me one day, as he'd pledged. Because of this love, I refused all offers of marriage, I remained a burden on my family, and my heart and mind and body have so burned with unrequited desire that I have failed to give to God the devotion that is his due.'

John could barely speak to say the words of absolution. He watched with dismay the frailty with which the woman rose from her knees and walked, almost tottering, from the chapel, having betrayed no sign that she knew who he was. For hours afterwards he sat there. She'd kept faith to their pledge after all, she'd never ceased to wait for him, and he perceived what toll her lovesickness had taken on her strength, as she'd not had the solace he'd found in the monastic routine of study and prayer. What might have been! It was unbearable to contemplate. You might say it was not too late; they could still find love in these late years. But it was a sacred bond that John had made with God. His renunciation of the flesh was absolute.

In truth, though, it really was too late. Not many days later he was summoned by Sir Nicholas Poyntz, grandson of Sir Robert, to attend a dying person at Acton Court. In great consternation, hoping against hope it might be some aged retainer who'd run life's natural course, John rode out to that manor to which he'd come in the King's train all those years before. When he arrived the steward told him in sombre tones that death had beaten him to the door. He was shown into the chamber where Mary Poyntz lay pale and still in her bed. In death the lines in her face had softened so she looked almost as youthful as he remembered her.

By her bed was a letter addressed to 'the Master of the Gaunts' Hospital'. Had she known him after all when she came to confession? Dripping tears on the parchment, he opened the seal. The letter contained only a formal request: 'I wish to be buried in the Poyntz chapel, dressed in a white silk gown that may be found in my wardrobe and has never been worn, and that in my hair be placed the pin enclosed with this letter.' John upturned the envelope. Into his trembling hand fell the gold bodkin he'd given her when they'd pledged their undying love.

He buried her as she instructed, in the chantry chapel, dressed in her wedding gown, the bodkin in her hair. Ever afterwards he made his private devotions in that chapel. He prayed for Mary's soul, and in the secrecy of his heart he prayed to her as well, as if she were his God, and begged her forgiveness for his lack of faith.

Even such a private matter of the heart is not immune to the tides of history. Once he'd broken with Rome, Henry VIII was eager to seize the lands and wealth of England's monasteries. On 9 September 1539, John Coleman surrendered the Gaunts' Hospital to the King's commissioners and was paid off with a pension. He would have had a kind welcome back in the monastery on the Rhine, but instead he took a cottage in Gaunts Lane so that he might always be near Mary. There he lived to a great age, cultivating his little garden behind the church in which the body of his beloved Mary lay.

Thirteen

THE BOGGLEWORT

If you go for a stroll on Robinswood Hill you may not realise that in the twisted caverns beneath your feet lives the King of the Boggleworts, and that in the network of passages that spread out from there for miles many hundreds of other boggleworts lurk. Unseen by night, underground, among the trees and shadows, they do their work. They cause the grass to grow, the leaves to bud, the flowers to unfurl, the grain to ripen, the apples to swell, the water to rise in springs and wells, the birds' eggs to develop, the cows' udders to fill, the sheep's fleeces to thicken. Their work goes on every night, on every farm, and all they want as thanks is cream from the milk, put out on a saucer last thing at night. You see, they need that cream to make their beards grow. They're hairy fellows as a rule – even the womenfolk – but it's their beards that are their pride and joy. Every Midsummer's Night the boggleworts gather inside Robinswood Hill; at midnight they emerge from a hole among the brambles and stand beneath the stars to see who has the longest, most beautifully comb-sculpted beard.

A certain bogglewort lived on a farm in that hamlet which so delighted Charles II, after a draughty night on Painswick Beacon

during his flight from Worcester, that he named it 'Paradise'. The farm had its eccentricities: besides the usual crops and livestock, there was a row of pomegranate trees and in one steep paddock a flock of llamas. So the bogglewort was a bit of a specialist, skilled in such tasks as getting pomegranates to ripen and llamas' wool to lengthen. He did his work without complaining and each night the farmer's wife put out a saucer of cream to keep his beard healthy and long. There were hedgehogs about who'd have a go at the cream if they got the chance, but so long as the bogglewort was quick he got his cream, and the hedgehogs, who weren't fussy, found other things to eat.

All was well until the farmer's wife was taken ill. She didn't want to grizzle, she played down that it could be anything serious, but serious it was and, as she lay dying, she said to her husband, 'Don't be silly and sentimental, my love. I know you've always been true to me, but you'll get in a pickle if you try to run this place by yourself, so once I'm gone – don't be shy – get down to Gloucester and find yourself a new wife.'

With that blessing, the farmer went down to the city as soon as she was dead. He knew exactly where to go. In the churchyard behind St Mary de Crypt there's a semicircular stone bench carved with the features of such beings as you might see in nightmares or dreams. They say that, in times past, a sage of great wisdom told tales at this bench to anyone who would come to listen. Whether tales are told there still, who knows, but it's certainly a place where young people may gather after dark to posture and flirt and utter loud ape-like cries. At a certain time of the week it's known that young women who wish to get hitched will come and sit on that bench and so bypass the usual confusion that attends English courtship.

When the farmer arrived he saw five women on the bench. Now let us be straight; in questions of sexual attraction there's a ruthlessness of judgement that can't be denied. The first woman was – in this man's eyes, if not another's – too fat. The second was too thin and bony. The third had piercing sad eyes that made his heart sink. The fourth ... well, the fourth was very good-looking indeed and he didn't have the nerve to speak to her. The fifth, however, had a spark of willing conversation; there was a tit for tat between them, which he liked, and she was nice enough in the other ways that matter.

So he said, 'Will you marry me?' and she said, 'Yes, I will,' and he took her home to his farm in Paradise. She loved it there: the view across Painswick Valley to the woods of Saltridge Hill; the flowers that filled the garden and meadow in the spring; and she adored the llamas with their tufty hairdos and long-lashed eyes. She was useful enough in the house, and did her best on the farm; but she was born and bred a city girl and she didn't believe there were such things as boggleworts.

At first she did put out the cream, as the farmer had instructed, but she knew it was hedgehogs that were drinking it; one night she even caught one in the act. It seemed a waste of good cream. Without a word to her husband, she took to putting out less cream and making up the difference with ordinary milk. If that led to any consequence it was nothing they noticed. Then she kept back the cream entirely and put out just a saucer of milk, which went just as readily as before. But the farmer did start to notice things amiss. It wasn't much – just that the hens were producing fewer eggs, and the cows less milk, and there was a rancid taste to the water from the well – and he didn't think much of it. His wife didn't perceive any problem. To save wasting milk, she watered down the amount she put out. The little things gradually became bigger things. The llamas developed a skin infection. There was a plague of slugs in the carrots. The bluebells under the trees shrivelled before they'd properly opened.

Midsummer's Night was a lovely clear night, bright with stars and a gibbous moon. But sometime after midnight the farmer's wife heard a shrieking and howling from the woods, and crashes and bangs, like some spectral replay of a battle long ago, and she clung in fear to her husband's snoring form. In the morning the farm looked as though there really had been a battle. The vegetables were trampled, the hens' eggs were smashed, the llamas and cows were stranded in the treetops, the well was soiled with dung, and the new pomegranates and apples had been ripped from the branches and stamped on the ground.

The farmer stared in consternation at the mess. He turned to his wife. 'Have you been putting out fresh cream regular each night for the bogglewort?'

'I don't believe there's any bogglewort.'

'Have you been putting out the cream?'

'Well … yes and no.'

The farmer wrung from her the truth that all she'd put out lately was watered-down milk. 'Whatever it was, it drank it just the same.'

'That'll be the hedgehogs as drank it. Don't you realise what's happened? Without cream the bogglewort's beard won't grow. Last night was Midsummer's Night, when the boggleworts compete with their beards on Robinswood Hill. Our bogglewort won't have had any beard worth showing. You've made him the laughing stock of them all.'

The farmer's wife burst into tears. 'I don't believe in boggleworts, but I can see there's something unnatural about this place. It may be called Paradise, but I don't like it here any more and I want us to leave.'

'What? Leave the farm?'

'Yes, let's sell up and go somewhere far away where you can take a new farm.'

The farmer wanted his wife happy, and she knew how to be persuasive, so he sold up the farm – buildings, fields, gardens, cattle, chickens, llamas, and all. They loaded their boxes and furniture on a wagon and drove off through Gloucester, past the Malverns, all the way north to their new farm in Shropshire.

The farmer strode around his new yard, eyeing up the state of things, what work had to be done. The wife began to unload boxes from the wagon. Suddenly she froze. Rising up from behind a cupboard at the back was a small wizened being. His limbs were covered with bristly hair, his pate was bald, and on his chin was a thin layer of fuzz. His deep-set eyes transfixed the woman with a fierce, unblinking gaze.

The wife screamed. The farmer came running. He saw the little figure on the trailer – and laughed. 'What are you doing here?'

'What do you reckon?' said the bogglewort in a voice like splintering wood. 'I can't never show my face anigh Robinswood Hill no more, so what could I do but come with you? Anyroad, how you going to run a farm without no bogglewort to make things grow?'

Fourteen

TEGAU
GOLDEN~BREAST

One sunset when Caradog, a prince of Gwent, was visiting Cirencester on royal business, he walked outside the city walls and chanced upon the ancient mound they call Tar Barrow. He heard voices conversing in a musical tongue he couldn't understand, and then saw between the beeches a woman and a man of unearthly beauty, their hair like gold in the sun's last light. He was smitten instantly by the woman's beauty. In the same moment that he knew he loved her, his heart was broken by the obvious fact she loved this other man.

When they saw him, the man studied him with a piercing green gaze, then turned and disappeared into the twilight. The woman waited with a shy smile that seemed to express, just as Caradog felt, the recognition that here was the other soul each had been waiting all their life to meet.

'But …' Caradog gestured where the other man had been standing.

'My brother. Dreon map Nudd.'

Her own name was Tegau. She gave Caradog her love that very night. The very next day, though he hardly knew her, though she seemed too gracious and lovely to belong in this world, he married her.

Not long afterwards, at Pentecost, Caradog and his new bride attended King Arthur at Caerleon with the other kings and knights and ladies. Just as the feast was to be served, a stranger entered the hall: a tall imposing fellow in his middle years, who wore the tonsure of a druid and a long green cloak. In his hands was a long, curved ox horn with a golden rim.

'Welcome, and tell us what adventure you bring,' said Arthur, who always hoped for some marvel to enliven this feast day.

'I bring you a gift.' The druid, whose name was Eliavrés, spoke with the accent of Armorica. 'This horn carries an enchantment to test the trust between man and wife. It will suffer no man to drink from it who has cause to doubt the fidelity of his wife, whether in deed of body or impulse of mind.'

All the married ladies present, even the High Queen, looked down at the floor. So did some of the men. The unmarried maidens giggled behind their hands.

'I for one have no cause to fear this challenge,' said the High King.

He took the horn, had it filled with wine, but when he tried to drink, the wine spilled down his gold-brocaded robe. Queen Guinevere hid her blushing face. The maidens choked not to laugh. King Arthur, beetroot red, loudly demanded, 'Let every married man here try the test of this horn!'

Whether king or knight, old or young, not one of them could get any wine from that horn down his throat and not his clothes. Till at last it was the turn of Caradog, the most newly married. He looked to his lovely Tegau and realised how little he yet knew the character of his wife.

'You may drink without fear, my love,' she said.

He put the horn to his lips, tipped it, and sweet wine ran smoothly on his tongue. There was a stiff silence of envy through the hall. Then King Arthur got possession of his manners and began to applaud. 'At least there's one among us who can hold his drink!' The hall erupted with laughter and applause. 'And has a fine wife worthy of him. Will you tell us, lady, from whence you hail?'

'From Cirencester.'

'A fair city – and one in need of a lord of character to hold it against the Saxon peril.' Arthur turned to Caradog. 'Your father may be king in Gwent but it's time you had lands of your own. I give you Cirencester and its lands southwards.' And to Tegau: 'You I give this horn as tribute to your faithfulness.'

Then Eliavrés, the druid, spoke up on pretext of Caradog having won the trial of the horn, and asked to speak with him in private.

Once they were outside the hall he said, 'Your wife may be faithful now, young man, but I warn you be on your guard. Who can know where the winds of love will blow?'

Caradog was outraged. 'How do you dare say such a thing?'

'Because, though you do not know me, I am your father.'

The words hung upon the silence. Till Caradog cried, 'My father is the King of Gwent!'

'Not so. Your mother is, like me, Armorican; it may have been because we were both exiles in a new land that we were drawn to each other. While her husband was campaigning in the north she became my lover and you, my son, were conceived.'

'You lie!' But Caradog knew in his bones that Eliavrés spoke the truth, that this man was indeed his natural father.

The King of Gwent, who'd raised Caradog as his son, was old and ailing and had not come to Caerleon. When the feast was finished, Caradog rode straight to the royal castle at Caerwent and confronted his mother, Queen Ysave, who was younger than her husband and still a lovely woman.

'Try to understand, my son. I was lonely and my husband was often away fighting. And Eliavrés is a master of enchantment. I was powerless to resist him, so I thought at first, though later I came to love him deeply.'

'Later? How long did this carry on?'

'I have said enough. Remember that I have stood by my husband … I have loved him in a way.'

Caradog had guessed the worst. In a rage at his mother's wantonness, he stormed to the chamber of the old King and told him as much as he thought he should know. Who can say how that hurt the old man's spirit, or how much he'd already guessed? Having exacted the King's consent, Caradog took Queen Ysave under guard to Cirencester and imprisoned her high in a tower of the Silchester Gate to keep her from Eliavrés' clutches.

He reckoned without the powers of the druid, who by concealing his material body as he climbed the winding stairs soon won his way into Ysave's prison and comforted her with his love. Yet it was beyond even his enchantments to spirit her away from a stronghold so well guarded. The two plotted instead some means by which to put their son in their power.

One day when Tegau had gone to Tar Barrow to meet her enigmatic brother, Caradog went to the tower to see Ysave, for she was still his mother and it was his duty to attend to her needs. He found her with hair uncombed and in clothes so grimy it looked as though she hadn't changed for days.

'Do you have no comb, no fresh clothes?'

'What does it matter what I look like if no one who loves me can see me? I feel too heart-weary in this prison to do anything.'

It cut Caradog to the quick to hear his mother speak so. 'Then I will bring your clothes and comb. Tell me where to find them.'

Limply she gestured to the wardrobe. Caradog opened the door, plunged his hands among the folded gowns – then screamed as something bit his left hand. He snatched his hand back to see a snake attached to it by the fangs. Its muscular body was coiled round the length of his arm. However he struggled, he could not loosen the reptile's grip. The tower guards couldn't help him. It was as if the snake had grafted itself upon his flesh. From its jaws clamped to his hand it sucked his blood. Its coils around his arm constricted tighter and tighter.

Caradog feared lest Tegau should see him so afflicted. He fled from the gatehouse to spend the night in the woods. By the morning his arm had withered within the snake's coils and he felt enfeebled beyond his years. He could not bear the thought of Tegau seeing him; he couldn't believe she'd still love him. He fled into the swampy wastes of the upper Thames and wandered there many days, the snake thickening upon his arm, till he came to a lonely shrine and a stone cell where an old hermit lived.

The hermit listened patiently as Caradog told him what had happened and bewailed the lack of love he'd shown his mother. 'For always she loved me, and tried to be loving to her husband, and was true to her love for Eliavrés even if that love were offence to law and sanctity.'

The hermit prayed for Caradog and cared for him in his humble cell. Yet the snake remained, a constant impediment and tribulation, which the prince endured for month after month, till two whole years had passed.

In the meantime, Tegau grieved for his absence. The soldiers she sent out combed the marshes in vain, yet she could not believe her Caradog was dead. So she went to Tar Barrow to call upon her brother Dreon map Nudd and his knowledge of the wild.

Diligently, Dreon scouted through the mires and the woods, but it was intractable terrain, where mists clung close to the swampy earth and it was easy to miss such a tiny thing as a hermit's cell. For month after month he searched, till at last he discovered the old hermit drawing water from a stream. The hermit took him to the missing prince. Dreon was shocked to see the bloated reptile coiled round Caradog's arm and him so gaunt and grim as if all the sap had been sucked out of him.

When Dreon told him that Tegau yet longed for him, he said, 'I cannot go back and let her see me in this state.'

So Dreon returned alone to Cirencester. It seemed to him that, if Caradog's salvation could be won, the place to start was the tower where his mother was incarcerated and the snake had struck. It was after dark when Dreon came there. Silent-footed in the manner of his kind, he climbed the spiral stairs. In the chamber he heard low voices. He caught them together in the bed: Ysave – the Queen of Gwent – and that canny druid.

The two men studied each other. Both sensed a kind of kinship in that neither of them was entirely of this mortal world.

Dreon said, 'What would it take to free your son from the snake's enchantment?'

'My price to tell you is the freedom of Queen Ysave.'

'If you will trust that I speak in Caradog's name, then I promise she shall be free.'

'For the snake to be dispelled,' said Eliavrés, 'will require the courage and loyalty of a woman who loves Caradog more than she loves her own body.'

'Tell me what such a woman would have to do?'

And Eliavrés instructed Dreon in everything that was necessary. Then Dreon went to his sister and told her all – about Caradog and his affliction and what must be done to cure it. Tegau's face turned pale when she heard what that cure was, but she said, 'I will do it.'

Together they rode into the marshes, to the hermit's cell. When Caradog learnt that Tegau had come, he tried to hide. She would not let him. She lifted his face in her hands and made him look into her eyes. 'I love you, Caradog, as much as that first evening we met on the barrow. Body and soul I love you.'

With the hermit's help, Dreon prepared everything as Eliavrés had said: one tub filled with vinegar and two sword's lengths away another filled with milk. Caradog took off his clothes and, with the huge bloated snake upon his arm, lowered his emaciated body into the tub of vinegar. Tegau stripped off her clothes in turn and lowered her lovely plump body into the tub of milk and rested one succulent white breast on the rim. In the cool open air the nipple swelled long and firm. Her brother stood ready with his sword.

Softly then Tegau spoke: 'O serpent, look to my soft young breast. That man is withered and drained. Nothing remains there to feed you. But I am soft and ripe and full of sap. My breast waits to nourish you.'

The snake felt the sting of vinegar between its scales and smelt the fresh milk in which the woman sat; it throbbed to the rhythm of her voice and eyed the tasty offering on the tub rim. Suddenly it pulled its fangs from Caradog's hand, uncoiled from his arm, and sprang, jaws agape, across the gap. Dreon was quick. The sword slashed down. But the snake was so swift, the nipple was in its jaws, the woman screamed, the blade sliced off

the serpent's head and with the same blow cut the nipple from Tegau's breast.

As the blood spilled down the milky skin, and Tegau wept in shock, the hermit applied a poultice of herbs to staunch the flow. When at last the wound was dressed, Caradog took his wife in his arms.

'I thank you with all my heart, that you've freed me from my curse. Yet what a price you have paid!'

'It is but one small piece of my body to buy the wholeness of yours.'

Healed, and reunited with his Tegau, Caradog returned to Cirencester, where he released his mother from the tower and begged her forgiveness for his lack of love. As time went by, he gradually recovered his strength. With daily exercise even the muscles of his withered left arm regrew – and so his friends gave him the name 'Freichfras', which means 'Strong-Arm'.

News came that the King of Gwent had died. In what state of heart that old man died, the stories don't say. King Arthur summoned Caradog and Tegau to Caerleon, as Caradog was named heir to his foster-father's title and lands.

In the Forest of Dean the High King took Caradog and other guests hunting. They pursued a boar into a rocky winding labryinth of scowles, but then rain came, and thunder, and Caradog got separated from the rest. Amidst the driving rain and the midday dark of thunderclouds, he beheld what seemed a glade of sunshine within the storm, in which the birds were singing and in the centre of which rode a green-cloaked man. Caradog spurred his horse to follow him. The bubble of sunshine and birdsong moved with them, deeper into the forest, by paths Caradog would never have found by his own skill, till they reached a wooden lodge, turf roofed, in a flowery clearing through which a brook trickled.

The stranger welcomed Caradog indoors, where a fire crackled in the hearth, and a young man played on a harp, and raven-haired women took the visitor's cloak and boots. From beyond a curtain of silk appeared an older woman, so beautiful, so gorgeously attired in an emerald gown, that Caradog didn't know her at first. His mother, Ysave. And then he realised that the man he'd followed here was none other than his father, Eliavrés.

So Caradog stayed as guest of his father and mother; he stayed some time. It was easy to lose track of time in that secluded lodge, and there was much to be shared – spoken and unspoken – among the three of them. Caradog felt glad to see how radiantly his mother smiled, how the lines in her face softened, in the company of the man she loved; and yet he could not forget the price his Tegau had paid.

Perhaps Eliavrés knew that unspoken thought. He showed his son an antique shield whose wood was splintering but whose boss was tipped with incorruptible gold. 'This gold carries an enchantment to mould to any surface on which it's placed.' He sought understanding in Caradog's eyes. 'Would you like it as a gift?'

With that nub of gold in his bag, Caradog returned to Caerleon. In the outside world more days had passed than he'd noticed in the forest. Tegau fell upon him, weeping. 'O my love! I thought I'd lost you again!'

Alone with her in private, he asked her to uncover her breasts. Shyly, silently, she obeyed. Caradog took the nub of gold and placed it on the scar. She gasped at the cool of the metal, then gasped again as it morphed into an exact replica of the missing nipple, but made of gleaming yellow gold.

'Let this be a secret between us,' said Caradog, 'in honour of your faithfulness.'

But I guess the secret got out, as it wasn't long before Tegau acquired the name 'Eurfron', meaning 'Golden-Breast'. So she has been known ever since: Tegau Eurfron, one of the Three Faithful Wives of the Island of Britain; and the love between her and Caradog Freichfras is one of the Three Bonds of Enduring Love.

Fifteen

THE OLD MEN
OF PAINSWICK

The village of Painswick was long known for the purity of its air and the good health of its inhabitants. That was before the coming of the motorcar and things like cigarettes and hamburgers and sugary snacks. One day, long ago, a pilgrim was trudging up the road from Stroud. No one knows what kind of pilgrim he was or what destination he was heading to beyond Painswick, only that he was a godly man who'd placed his hope in going to heaven after he died. You might say that heaven was his true destination.

As he got in sight of the steeple of Painswick Church, he came upon an old man sitting on a pile of stones by the roadside. The pilgrim had wandered far and wide on his travels and never had he seen a man who looked quite so old. What's more, the fellow was crying his eyes out.

'Hush, old chap. What's the matter?'

'It be my father!' wept the old man. 'He gived me such a walloping!'

'Your father?'

'Yes sure, I comed down hither to get away from he.'

How could a man so old have a father? Surely his father had been dead and buried a century! The old codger must have got a bit raddled in the head.

But the pilgrim, being a do-gooding godly fellow, wanted to help him in his misery. He offered to carry him home on his back. That wasn't too great a labour, as the old man's body was little more than skin, string and bones.

The pilgrim carried him up past the church to the ancient stone cottage that the old man said was his home. Waiting at the gate into the yard was an old, old man, even older than the first. He was stooping so low that his long white beard almost brushed the ground. In his hands was a stout stick. The pilgrim, as he lowered the first old man from his back, guessed who this must be.

'Sir, please put down your stick. Why do you beat your son who's attained so ripe an age?'

'He do need a good larroping!' warbled the old father. 'Dubbing stones he were at my father whilst he were up the apple tree!'

'Your father?'

'Aye, he do be up there yet.'

In the garden was a big straggly apple tree that looked well overdue for a trim. There was a ladder against it, and high in the branches an old, old, old man, even older than the last one, puffed and groaned as with a trembling hand he plucked apples to put in his basket.

The pilgrim was horrified to see a man of such great age so precariously perched. 'Are you all right up there, old chap? Shall I help you come down?'

'I has to pick they apples,' panted the old man. 'My father do need they to bake an apple pie.'

'Your father?'

'Yes sure, he be a solid cook … Shall 'ee bide with we for dinner?'

Appetising smells were indeed wafting from the kitchen. The pilgrim had been walking all day and was feeling quite peckish, and he'd learnt to accept the fruits of providence in whatever unlikely places they fell. He stooped hesitantly under the lintel into the kitchen. There, sure enough, wearing an

apron, tortuously rolling out pastry, was an old, old, old, old man. The pilgrim had never imagined that anyone could look so very old.

'Sir, your – er – son suggested that perhaps I might stay for dinner.'

The old man worked his gummy jaws till he managed to force out some words: 'I bain't sure about such ... I just be the cook ... Thee shalt have to ask my father ...'

'Your father?'

The man worked his jaws again and made a shaky gesture. 'Aye ... he do be in the parlour ...'

The pilgrim stepped, disbelieving, into the next room. Sitting in a rocking chair was an old, old, old, old, old man, so very ancient that his features were almost lost in the wrinkles and the only sign of hair was a faint white tuft on his chin.

'If I may,' said the pilgrim, 'I wanted to ask if I might stay for dinner.'

Slowly, tremulously, the old man turned his head. 'Whassat?'

The pilgrim spoke a bit louder: 'Would it be all right if I stayed for dinner?'

'What b-b-be that … as … thee … b-b-bist a-saying?' quavered the patriarch.

'Can I Stay For Dinner, Please?'

'That … do … depend …' The pilgrim had to stoop close to make out the words. 'It … d-d-do … depend … according as … thee c-c-canst … eat … quiet-like … so thee d-d-doesn't … wake up … my … f-f-father …'

'You have a father?'

'Anunst … in the box.'

Box?

On the mantelpiece stood a carved ivory box. The pilgrim went to look. Inside the box, eyes closed, arms and legs curled up like a baby's, was a tiny shrivelled old man, far older yet than any of the others. Suddenly this ancient one's eyes opened and glared fiercely up. In their depths the pilgrim perceived a bottomless melancholy that seemed to encompass all things.

'On second thoughts,' he said briskly, 'I think I best be on my way. I have quite a distance to travel.'

And he scooted out of that parlour, out of the kitchen, out of the yard, and out of the village of Painswick, as quick as he could go. He dared not stay any longer. He was, as I said, a godly man, who'd placed his hope in going to heaven after he died. He was afraid that if you stayed too long in Painswick then you might never die.

Sixteen

WHITE LADY'S GATE

One of the terrible things about civil wars is the way they make mortal enemies of people who've lived side by side all their lives. So it was in Gloucestershire during the Great Rebellion against King Charles. John Morris of Chipping Campden was a Puritan who took Parliament's side. Sir Roger Northwick, who'd learnt his letters from the minister alongside John's sister Beatrice, fought for the King. When Parliament was triumphant and the King had been executed, John was rewarded with prestigious office as a magistrate. Sir Roger, who'd beggared his fortune for the Royalist cause, now forfeited also his lands. No choice was left to him that his pride could bear but to turn highwayman. His beat was the high road between Broadway and Stow. Dressed all in black, with a mask across his face, and mounted on a black charger, he became notorious as the enigmatic 'Black Knight'.

Late one evening a stagecoach was rattling northwards up that road, when a horseman erupted from the shadows. As the highwayman aimed his pistols at the driver and guard, and waited for the purses to be thrown out, he glimpsed among the dark figures in the coach a pale form caught by the moonlight: a pallid

face, a white cloak around the shoulders, a white coif over black
bound hair. He saw the cloak slip as the woman unfastened her
brooch and passed it out. It was silver, crafted in the shape of a
dove in flight.

'Let the lady keep her brooch,' said the highwayman. 'I would
not want her to catch a chill for want of a pin for her cloak.'

When she heard the man's voice, Beatrice Morris recognised it.
She'd known that voice since it had been a boy's, unbroken. As
the brooch returned to her hand, her eyes met the robber's above
the mask and it seemed to her then that he knew what she knew.
It was one of those moments that last an instant in reality and
yet feel immense, a glimmering void of uncertainty of what is
known and what is felt and what it all might mean.

The highwayman vanished into the night. The coach rattled
on to the Cross Hands, where John Morris was waiting to take
his sister home. He was furious to discover the Black Knight had
struck again and Beatrice had been at his mercy. She, meanwhile,
pondered the power over a man's life which she now possessed –
which seemed entrusted to her by the recognition she'd detected
in his eyes. She had no sympathy for any Royalist cause that
would defend a king's tyranny against the rights of common folk,
but to think of Sir Roger Northwick condemned to the gallows
made her reel with horror; it crystallised in her heart something
dormant since her childhood. Beatrice was a woman past thirty
and never married, for all that she was beautiful and gracious.
That night it broke upon her like a devastating storm how her
heart's destiny had been biding its time all these long years of
loneliness and war.

Day and night she brooded upon him. She reasoned he must
have a safe house somewhere near among his Royalist friends.
She guessed which house that might be and worked out the route
by which he would travel from there to the Stow road to begin
his night's work. A month went by. The blackthorn blossomed; the
bluebells and celandines bloomed. All of creation was quick with
life when Beatrice slipped away one evening from her brother's
house and rode up Dyer's Lane to Dover's Hill. She hobbled her

horse and stood high up the hillside, in view of the lane, to wait with pounding heart till she heard the clip-clop of a rider ascending the lane from Weston. She freed her white silk cloak and swung it above her head so the moonlight reflected from its shimmering folds. When the hoof beats fell silent, she ran down to the gate.

There he was, her masked Black Knight, hesitant at first, till he recognised her. Then, in one agile movement, he vaulted from the saddle and over the gate.

'So it was you, that night?' he said.

'Yes, Roger.'

Beatrice saw how he flinched to hear his name. For a moment her heart failed her. She regarded the long sword at his hip.

He said, 'All this past month I've been thinking of you.'

In the next moment they were in each other's arms and everything Beatrice had hoped, and guessed, and felt deep inside proved true, only stronger than she'd ever imagined. They kissed with a passion that perhaps can only be known in the shadow of war and death. Hand in hand, they ran down the moonlit sward, where sheep lay like fluffy boulders, lambs cuddled against them. In the secrecy of the woods below, speared by shards of moonlight through the branches, invigorated by the smell of budding leaves, they kissed hard and deep, they whispered hot words of love, they held each other close. Till Beatrice knew she must be home before anyone wondered where she was.

'You'll speak not a word?' he said.

'Your secret is safe with me.'

'You'll come again?'

'I shall, my love. Look for my white cloak in the moonlight and meet me at the gate.'

On fair moonlit nights throughout the halcyon weeks of spring, Beatrice would ride to Dover's Hill and wave her white silk cloak and meet Sir Roger at the gate, and beneath the trees' thickening foliage they would kiss and caress, and declare their love, and dream of what their lives could yet be.

'Give me a twelvemonth and with luck I'll have won silver enough for us to take ship for France, away from this torn land,

and there we'll be man and wife and live the good life that God desires for us all.'

Beatrice loved him so much that his dream was her prayer and she put from her mind the trade by which her beloved earned his silver on the highway. She betrayed not a syllable about her secret love, for she knew the mind of her brother – how he saw himself as her keeper despite her years – and the bitterness engrained in him and his Puritan kin by the war's barbarity. Each time she slipped away at dusk she took care not to be observed.

But not quite enough. As an officer in the war, John had become a sharp-witted man. He noticed his sister's evening absences. He became watchful. One evening in May, when the moon was near full in a sky yet blue, he hid behind a hedge of trees and observed Beatrice steal to the stables and then ride off with a fierce eagerness in her face. His conscience clamoured at the moral peril in which he feared she'd fallen. He saddled his stallion and followed her at a distance where she wouldn't hear his horse's hooves.

From the thorn trees along the lane he saw her white cloak shimmy on the hillside. He saw the black-garbed horseman alight near the gate and how she came rushing to embrace him. He saw the man pull the mask from his face to kiss her. Roger Northwick! So that Royalist dastard was the Black Knight who haunted the highways to rob honest men – and shamelessly made free with John's own sister! The Puritan's heart burnt with righteous rage. The fact that Roger was armed to the teeth, that it would be too dangerous to act alone, made John's anger boil all the worse. Quietly he slipped away. Now the truth was known he would see justice done and his sister liberated from sin.

No doubt he presumed that the sin of sins had already been done. The truth that evening was that Beatrice Morris, at thirty-two years of age, was yet a virgin. The woods were warm, the nightingales singing, wood pigeons cooing; the air was heady with pollen and scent. She knew no more than any of us ever do about what the future held; yet maybe there is a deeper consciousness of the patterns of life and death than our senses or reason can perceive. That night her body and soul were liquid with love. Roger caught it in her eyes, in the trembling of her lips, in the shiver of static in the air. On the winding path through the trees he paused in his stride, beheld Beatrice walking ahead, her cloak shining silver like an elf queen's in the moonlight. He glanced back and it seemed to him that the path curving away behind was all the pilgrimage through the years that had brought them from their lessons with the minister to this moment of love as full as the swollen moon.

He said, 'I would that you be right now my wife in the wood.'

She turned with a beaming smile. 'Is this your formal proposal of marriage?'

'Proposal, aye, and the very vow if you'll have me.'

There in the spring wood, as much a house of God as any building of stone, with nightingales their witnesses, the trees their congregation, the moonbeams their blessing, the Royalist lord and the Puritan maiden gave each other all their love; like Adam and Eve before the time of tears began.

In the days afterwards Beatrice was too brimming with happiness to notice anything unusual in her brother John's manner towards her. But the next fine evening, when she was saddling the mare to ride out, he appeared at the stable door. His face was cold as winter. Without a word of explanation he took her white silk cloak.

'What are you doing?' she cried.

Without a word of reply he handed her over to their uncle to be imprisoned in his house while John, with a posse of troopers who'd ridden with him to battle, rode up Dyer's Lane to Dover's Hill. He set the men in wait among the thorn trees and climbed alone up the sward. When he heard the hoof beats approaching, he waved the cloak above his head so it caught the golden light of the setting sun.

When Sir Roger dismounted by the gate he saw no sign of his beloved. Instead a squad of fully armed Roundheads leapt from the shadows on every side. He drew his sword to fight, but

there were too many blades to parry. John seized his moment and ran him through the heart. The Black Knight crumpled to the ground and with the last breath from his lips whispered Beatrice's name.

Beatrice lost her reason when they told her the news. She could not do the simplest tasks without a servant's help. For six months she was her uncle's prisoner. When they gave her back her liberty she stayed in his house; she would not return to her brother's. On the evening of the full moon in December, she went out to Dover's Hill. She wandered the rough sward in her white silk cloak and glanced down at the lane, the gate, as if expecting her Roger to appear.

The night was very cold. In the morning her body was found, stiff and pale, in the frosted grass a short way from the gate. They say that even today, on the night of the full moon, the ghost of Beatrice can be seen near that gate on Dover's Hill, forever glancing towards the lane, and that from her shoulders billows a long white cloak shimmering like mist in the moonlight.

Seventeen

St Kenelm
of Mercia

In the tumultuous age when England was divided into several kingdoms, crowns were readily contested and kings often met a violent and early death. A king would sometimes crown his heir as co-king to try to stabilise the succession in the event of his own sudden demise. So Kenulf, King of Mercia, who in the years after Offa had made Mercia pre-eminent among English kingdoms, crowned his son Kenelm co-king while yet a youth. Kenelm was a God-fearing young fellow, whom Kenulf was keen should rule after him in preference to his own devious brother, Ceolwulf.

One night, Kenelm had a dream in which he saw a tall tree grow beside his bed and bear a bright mass of blossom and fruit. He climbed to the top of this tree and saw below him the whole expanse of his kingdom, from the Severn to the Humber, the Ribble to the Thames. Then his best friend – in the dream it was unclear who that was – chopped down the tree and Kenelm transformed into a bird and flew to heaven.

Kenelm told the dream to his elder sister, Quenthryth, abbess of the minster their father had built in Winchcombe, his capital.

Her face turned pale as she listened. She was a woman who spent many hours in prayer and had some insight into what such manifestations of the inner life might portend.

'Why do you look so shocked?' young Kenelm asked.

'Because I fear this dream prophesies that someday your life will be threatened by treachery.'

Kenelm showed no fear. 'If that were so, it would be but a means by which I might follow more closely in the footsteps of our Lord.'

As it happened, the young king's life was indeed in peril. His uncle Ceolwulf was ambitious for the crown. He could not act against his brother, because Kenulf was a warrior of great size and strength and his housecarls were devoted to him. Kenelm was a softer target. By a campaign of flattery and promises Ceolwulf won the complicity of Kenelm's guardian, Ascebert, a man both learned and war-skilled, who had served him as both tutor and bodyguard. Ceolwulf corrupted him with hopes of wealth, high office and the hand in marriage of Abbess Quenthryth, for whom Ascebert had always had a lascivious affection. Ceolwulf encouraged him to flirt with her, and it seemed to Ascebert that she was responsive to his smiles and jokes. If the truth was that Quenthryth was committed to the life of a holy virgin and her warmth towards him was no more than a chaste indulgence of her womanly feelings, the seeming closeness between them was noticed.

When Ascebert proposed taking Kenelm to the royal hunting lodge in the Clent Hills, Quenthryth gave her blessing, since such a trip would remove the youth for a while from the hothouse of intrigue Ceolwulf had stoked up in Winchcombe. The lodge sat deep in the wilderness of woods that clothed the Clent Hills, where buck and boar roamed in plenty. It was steamy hot weather in which to chase game through arduous terrain. After a long fruitless pursuit of a boar on the second day, Kenelm lay down near the top of a wooded gully and slept. Ascebert seized his chance. Beneath a thorn bush he dug a pit; he had nearly finished when Kenelm awoke and saw it.

The young king looked at his trusted guardian and realised who the 'best friend' of his dream must be.

'You dig that grave in vain, because my body shall not sleep here but in a place many miles distant.' And to prove his words were prophecy Kenelm planted his staff in the earth and at once it took root and produced black buds which unfurled into leaves and flowers, and in a trice the staff had become a young ash sapling.

Ascebert drew a long, double-edged knife and crouched in fighting stance, expecting a struggle now the youth was awake. But Kenelm was one of those rare souls who truly take Jesus Christ at his word and example. He made no move to protect himself. Instead he quoted Jesus' words the night of his betrayal – 'What you're going to do, do it quickly' – and began to sing: 'We praise you, O God: we acknowledge you to be the Lord …'

Ascebert seized him and the song was silenced as he hacked off the youth's head. From the fountain of blood a white dove sprang and on quick, strong wing beats flew up into the sky. The murderer didn't see it. He flung the body, head and knife in the pit and quickly shovelled back the earth.

Buried beneath a thorn bush deep in a wooded wilderness the evidence would be hidden for ever, Ascebert hoped. Yet when he'd gone a shaft of sunlight pierced the treetops to illuminate the spot. So it shone every day. And a white cow, set loose each day by a poor widow who lived in the woods, found the place and munched the rich herbage growing there. When the cow came home in the evening her udder carried twice as much milk as any of the other cows'; when she returned to the gully in the morning the herbage was just as lush as before. The woodfolk perceived in all this some strange significance beyond their ken. They called the place 'Cowbach', which means 'Cow Vale'.

In Winchcombe, Ascebert reported, 'We got separated hunting a boar in dense forest … and Kenelm disappeared. I searched and searched, and called his name, over and over, but I could find no sign of him. I'm so sorry. The boar must have got him.'

Some believed him. Many didn't. How many royal heirs have died in mysterious hunting accidents? Ceolwulf put on a long face. Kenulf grieved. If some voices whispered malicious words about Quenthryth's friendship with Ascebert, the depth of her love for her little brother was plain. No one dared speak his name in her hearing for fear she'd break down in inconsolable tears.

Far away, in Rome, the Pope was singing Mass in St Peter's – when a white dove swooped before him and deposited a scroll on the altar. Once the service was finished, the Pope opened the scroll. Gold letters glittered from the vellum in a language he could not read. He called for scholars of every nation represented in Rome – Franks, Greeks, Asturians, Irish, Syrians – but it was an Englishman who solved the mystery, for the words were English:

> In Clent, Cowbach, Kenelm king-born
> lies under a thorn, his head off-shorn.

The Pope sent tidings of this miraculous message to the Archbishop of Canterbury, who sent word to King Kenulf. From Winchcombe a party of monks trekked north to the Clent Hills. They were daunted where to start looking in such a wilderness, but when they uttered the word 'Cowbach' to the woodfolk they were soon told where to go. Once they were near, a cow's mournful lowing guided them, and then the sunray spotlighting the buttercups and clover luxuriant beneath a hawthorn bush. There they dug, and found the body, the head, the blood-crusted knife. When they lifted Kenelm's body from the earth, a spring gushed from the spot and flowed down the gully. They built a chapel nearby and enshrined Kenelm's head inside it. His body they wrapped in a shroud and laid on a donkey's back to begin the journey home to Winchcombe.

By the time they reached Upton Snodsbury their progress was causing quite a stir. People flocked to see the body of the godly young king who'd been murdered. The blind, the lame, the deaf, the gout-ridden pressed near to touch it. Many were healed. So were many of those who drank from the spring where he'd been found. Word spread that this royal youth, who'd died blameless, a martyr of faith, had become a saint of the first order.

When the party stopped at Pershore Abbey, the resident monks were conscious of what a holy relic lay that very night in their church. They lay awake all night, contemplating the prestige such a relic would bring, the revenue from pilgrims, the fact that Kenelm had died at a location much closer to Pershore than to Winchcombe. The next day, as the Winchcombe monks struggled to get the donkey and its precious burden across the ford over the Avon, the Pershore monks arrived on the scene. They'd come not to help but to dispute possession of Kenelm's body. The situation became undignified. At one point all the monks were waist deep in the river, actually tugging the body from opposite ends. The donkey brayed and kicked. The monks heaved and wrestled. The water was so deep that some of the brothers got knocked right under.

'This won't do!' someone cried. 'Let's find a civilised way to decide what shall be done.'

The rest were too worn out to disagree. They all trooped back, with the body on the donkey, to Pershore Abbey. It was agreed that whichever party should wake first in the morning could claim possession of the corpse – a canny plan from the Winchcombe men's point of view, because the Pershore monks had slept so little the night before. While the latter slept deep, the Winchcombe brothers waited. They were up long before dawn – told themselves they'd 'woken first', though in truth they'd hardly gone to sleep in the first place – and stole away with Kenelm's body. They went not to Pershore's ford, where the local brothers might catch them as they struggled across the deep water, but instead hiked five miles upstream to Fladbury to cross the easier ford there.

When the Pershore monks woke at the crack of dawn and discovered the bird had already flown, they were furious. They raced to the ford. No sign of anyone there. Long gone, they thought, till a cowherd said she'd seen a party of monks with a donkey heading along the Avon's north bank. The Pershore men guessed their rivals' plan. They waded the ford at Pershore – unencumbered by donkey or corpse – and raced to intercept those Winchcombe rogues before they were across the Fladbury ford. They were just too late. They caught sight of the fleeing monks hustling down a path into the woods; they gave chase, but in the winding woodland paths they soon lost the trail.

The Winchcombe monks pressed on post-haste, sweltering under their tunics, panting for breath, urging the donkey on. Down the Salt Way they travelled, by Ashton under Hill, Dumbleton, Toddington and Hailes. They didn't stop till they'd crested Salter's Hill and could see the tower of Winchcombe Abbey. Almost home! In the sheltered little valley of Sudeley they laid the body down on the ground to let the donkey rest. At once from that spot a spring gushed forth to quench their raging thirst.

In Winchcombe, Kenelm's body was greeted with a potent mix of sorrow and joy. In an upper room of the abbey, Quenthryth heard the applause and voices raised to sing a psalm. She saw from the window the shrouded form being carried through the gatehouse arch. Tears flooded from her eyes. She opened her psalter, meaning to join in the psalm, but was so distraught that she held the book upside down and could see nothing of the words through her tears. She wept with such passion that the tears falling from her eyes became tears of blood which stained the parchment page.

They buried Kenelm's body in a stone coffin in the abbey church. The bloodstained knife was buried with him, but not before it was identified as Ascebert's. Before they put him to death he babbled accusations against both Ceolwulf and Quenthryth. Ceolwulf spread sordid rumours about

Quenthryth's complicity in Ascebert's crime. But King Kenulf knew his daughter was a good and holy woman. He preserved her as abbess of Winchcombe and appointed her over two abbeys in Kent also.

When Kenulf died, in the year 821, he was buried beside his son. The suspicions about Ceolwulf were not forgotten and the ealdormen and clergy were reluctant to make him king. Only a victory against the Welsh won him the crown. His harsh and devious style of rule soon turned the ealdormen against him. They deposed him after a few months. Mercia quickly lost its pre-eminence among the English kingdoms, and never regained it.

In the years and centuries after Kenelm's death many miracles of healing were wrought by his relics, and by the springs that had appeared where his body touched the earth, and by prayers on his birthday, 17 July. After seven hundred years had gone by, and the Reformation ran like a firestorm through England's monasteries, Winchcombe Abbey was demolished so completely you might not know it had ever existed. But in 1815 an excavation of the minster's foundations uncovered two stone coffins. The larger contained the bones of a man who must have stood six foot six. The smaller contained the headless skeleton of a man of much slighter build, and a long knife transformed into brittle oxide. At the workmen's touch the bones and knife crumbled into dust, but the two coffins remain on view today in St Peter's Church in Winchcombe.

Eighteen

THE SNOW
FORESTERS'
MIST-GATE

One cold Christmas Eve a family of Gypsies was travelling up the long drag from Burford to Stow. The horses' hooves and the caravan wheels were skiddy on the icy road. Night was coming on when it started to snow again. Soon the flakes were falling so thick the horses faltered and, in the gloom of Idbury Wood, Da couldn't even see the edges of the road he was driving on. There was nothing for it but to pull over and pray the snowstorm would ease.

Door and windows tightly shut, they huddled round the stove while the storm howled in the trees and battered at their little cabin on wheels, making it shudder as if the timber it was built of could feel the cold. From all around came a whistling whine and a pattering like light fingers on the windows.

'It's like there's someone out there trying to get in,' said the lad.

'So there be!' cackled Granny. 'They be the snow foresters. They'll get in at us if they can, and breathe on us their ice-cold breath.'

A flurry of fine snow jetted through the crack between the half windows and half door and sprinkled to the floor.

Then the lad heard something else: a pitiful mewling the other side of that door.

'That's not a snow forester, is it?'

'For sure it be they!' cried Granny, whose old ears couldn't make out so high-pitched a sound.

The lad realised it was a cat caught in the storm and pleading to be let in. He pushed open the half door. There was a gust of chill wind and a shower of snow, then cries of uproar, and an ear-splitting wail from Babbi. The little cat, white like snow, darted in and leapt into the lad's lap. Da's strong arm yanked the door back.

'What are you playing at?' screeched Mam as she rocked her wailing infant. 'Throw that dirty animal out!'

Kitty's green eyes stared entreaty at the lad and he cuddled her close to warm her.

'Do you know, lad?' said Granny in a whisper like dead leaves. 'Talk to a kitty in rhyme on Christmas Eve and she might talk back.'

There came a sudden assault of wind, which slammed each side of the caravan in quick succession, and the half door flew open wide. There was a shivering icy blast, one of the lanterns blew out, and snow pelted everywhere, even sizzled in the stove. Da lunged to haul the door shut. He brushed the snow from his coat, looked at his family, and I guess he realised something was wrong but wasn't sure what it was.

Mam screamed: '*Where's Babbi?*'

Everyone looked at everyone else. Mam, Da, Granny, the lad – and the cat. No sign of the baby girl.

'Didn't you have her?' cried Da.

'She was right here!' wailed Mam.

They looked left and right, up and down, as if there might be somewhere in that cramped space she was hiding.

'The snow foresters,' wheezed Granny. 'They must have took her when the door were open.'

Da gave the lad an accusing stare. If you hadn't opened the door to let in that animal … He grabbed him by the collar. 'Come! We have to find her!'

Into the howling night went Da, Mam and the lad. They stumbled and slithered in the woods. Over and over they yelled Babbi's name. The air, thick with snowflakes, soaked up their shouts. Their lanterns revealed black trunks overgrown with ivy like hairy giants. Icy fingers of snow poked down the lad's collar, and caressed his forehead till the skin felt tight enough to split, and in the darkness all round him he could hear the snow foresters' whining and moaning.

Mam's shrieks for her baby got so hoarse she could shriek no more. Freezing and exhausted, they tumbled back inside the caravan. Granny watched with grim resignation, the cat watched too, as the father held the sobbing mother. Once Da had his breath, he plunged back outside to try again. Mam threw an extra rug around her shoulders and bustled after him. But surely by now the baby had been out in the cold too long.

The lad looked at Granny. Granny looked at the cat. The lad remembered what she'd said: 'Talk to a kitty in rhyme on Christmas Eve and she might talk back.'

The lad would have tried anything. 'O little kitty-cat, white not black, / will you help me get my sister back?'

In a voice so purry soft that only the lad could hear, the cat said, 'The snow foresters have taken her through the mist-gate and into the fairy hill. You must fetch her out before the Christmas bells ring. Put salt in your pocket, for protection, and then let's ride upon the cross on the donkey's back.'

'What donkey is that, / tell me, little cat?'

'The parson's donkey from Stow, who went a-wandering, got lost in the storm, and is standing right now on the road.'

Granny said nothing, just gazed at the stove, as the lad pinched some salt from the cupboard, lifted the cat inside his jacket, and went out into the storm. He could hear his parents' futile shouts in the woods. They couldn't see him. They couldn't stop him. He found the poor old donkey huddling under a tree. He slapped her sides to warm her, then jumped astride the holy cross on her back, and, with the cat cuddled against his belly, rode off up the road, steep and slippery in the dark. The snow foresters still moaned their wild cries, but maybe the salt and the donkey's cross helped keep them at bay, for the curtain of snowflakes thinned enough for the lad to see the way.

It was a long haul up that road. The lad thought it would never end. 'Tell me how we'll get inside that hill / to bring back Babbi out into the chill?'

'Just a little further,' purred the cat. 'The mist-gate is open while the snow foresters be out dancing. But soon they'll be back inside the earth and they'll close up the mist-gate so they can't hear the church bells.'

From out of the darkness before them appeared a fearsome black dog. Another unholy creature of the night? No, this dog was the church grim that guarded St Edward's Church in Stow. He'd come in search of the errant donkey, and spoke kindly to the lad: 'I'll use my powers to keep the gate open as long as I can. Be sure you don't get down from the donkey's cross; I'll pass the baby up to you. As soon as you have chance, sign the cross in salt on her face.'

Further up they climbed through the snow and dark, the lad upon the donkey's back, the white cat snug inside his jacket, and the church grim trotting along beside. As the ground levelled out, they turned off the Stow road on to a little path across Wyck Beacon. Ahead stood a snow-flocked mound, ringed by spiky hawthorns and crowned by three voluptuous beech trees. Flitting among the trees, faint flaky figures twisted and twirled to the

whistle and strum of the wind. Low between the hawthorns, among the squirming beech roots, was a shape of shimmering mist, like an eye upon its end, or the slit between parting lips.

Maybe it was the salt, maybe the donkey's cross, but the snow foresters didn't see the little party reach that gate of mist. The cat sprang into a hollow in the roots to keep guard. The lad peered through the swirling, shimmering mist into the mystery of the hill.

'So this is the mist-gate? / You're sure we're not too late?'

'It's up to you now,' said the cat, 'if you want your sister back.'

The church grim stood beside the mist-gate and raised his paws in spiritual skill. The mist thinned so you could see the hollow darkness beyond. The lad gripped tight the donkey's mane and urged her into the still dark space within the fairy mound. From walls and roof came a faint silvery light like particles of starlight. The more you looked, the more it seemed that this light was a sky and that if you were to wander far you might lose yourself in a whole vast world hidden beneath this hill. For a moment, or two, or three, the lad forgot his purpose, and all his desire was to leap from the donkey's back and run and dance and see what he might find.

But the salt was in his pocket. He stayed seated on the donkey's holy cross. And in that silvery gloom he heard a baby's whimper, saw the little bundle quivering on the ground. The grim's black shadow hustled by. He lifted up Babbi in his paws. The lad cuddled her close so she could feel his love and warmth.

'Be quick!' said the grim. 'I can't hold the gate open much longer.'

The lad urged the donkey back through the mist into the mortal night and the shivering nip of snow. There came a shriek like an angry gale and the snow flocked thicker about them. The little white cat yowled in alarm.

'The snow foresters have seen you!' barked the grim. 'Quick, to the church!'

The cat sprang up and sank her teeth into the donkey's tail. The donkey brayed in pain and broke into a gallop. The lad clung to its mane with one hand, to Babbi with the other, and with the cat swinging by its jaws from the donkey's tail, and the church grim racing beside them, and the snow foresters howling behind, they raced to the road and down the hill. Both donkey and grim knew the way. They travelled as fast as they could go, three miles down that road, the foresters' cold breath on their backs, till at last the fair stone buildings of Stow loomed amidst the snow. There was the square tower of St Edward's. Here the gate into the churchyard. A candle twinkled through the open doors of the porch, framed by the corded black trunks of two yews.

Into the porch the lad scrambled with Babbi, while the snow foresters wheeled and screamed. He dipped his finger in his pocket and signed the cross in salt on Babbi's face. The grim padded inside the church and moments later the bells in the tower began to ring. Christmas was come. The snow foresters' shrieks subsided into a thin whistle and they funnelled away up Wyck Beacon, back through the mist-gate, and into the fairy hill. The falling snow thinned to a dainty decoration of the night. The white cat curled up warm beside Babbi. The lad rubbed down the donkey and told her what a good beast she'd been.

Soon the snow had stopped completely. Not long after that a Gypsy caravan came chackling up the street to the church, as if drawn there in spite of everything by the jubilant Christmas bells. Da's face was pale and grim. Mam's was wrecked with weeping. How their faces changed when the lad stepped out cuddling Babbi in his arms. Mam wept again for joy. Granny peered out between the caravan's half windows and sagely nodded her grey head.

'It's that cat we have to thank,' said the lad.

He turned back to the spot in the porch where the cat had been, but the little white cat was gone.

'She was here just a second ago!'

Granny smiled a toothless smile. 'I'd say she were a fallen angel who was earning her way back to heaven.'

Nineteen

THE BUCKSTONE
AND THE
BRITANNIC PALACE

In the extreme west of the Forest of Dean, on the rim of a wooded scarp near Staunton, sits a huge boulder of conglomerate. This stone, the Buckstone, used to be balanced on a boss of bedrock so that when you gave it a push it would rock back and forth. That's before it was dislodged by a party of drunken Victorian acrobats. In ancient times the druids used this stone as an oracle, by observing which way it rocked in response to questions they posed.

When the kings of Britain learnt from spies across the Channel that the Romans had a covetous interest in this island and its treasures of ore, those kings and their druids came from north, west, east and south to a great assembly in these oak woods of Siluria to discuss how they might combat the expected invasion. At sunset the druids gathered around the rocking stone to ask it what must be done to win the gods' favour in the trial to come. From the stone's movements, settling this way, then that, the answer came: a blood sacrifice must be made in the time-honoured way – of the first warm-blooded creature the druids set eyes upon when they returned to the stone at dawn. What might it be? Fox? Stag? Partridge? Wren? When they came back next morning, the first creature they saw was neither beast nor fowl. It was a girl.

She was barely into her teens, though tall for her age, with clear milky skin and flame-red hair. She was sitting on the stone, above its pivot, so it swayed when she turned to see the druids' grim faces and sharpened sickles. They knew who she was, but it made no difference; the powers of the earth had to be appeased. They formed a circle round the stone. They invoked the spirits. The Archdruid of Mona washed her blade with spring water. The girl stood quivering beside the stone, entranced by the chanting and the sunlight sparkling on the dew. Two druids took her arms. A third pushed back her head to expose her thin white throat. Her eyes flared with terror but she did not fight. The Archdruid raised her sickle —

And a roebuck flew out from the trees, leapt right over the stone, and into the arms of the druids. There could be no doubt: it was a gift from the gods; the oracle had but tested their faith. So a buck was slaughtered in place of young Gwladys, daughter of King Gwythr of the Catuvellauni, fostered to his brother Arwîrac, who'd brought her with him to the assembly because of her interest in the deeper mysteries of druidry. That morning Gwladys drank deeper of those mysteries than she'd sought.

For days afterwards she had a heightened sensitisation to everything around her. The reprieve she'd been granted woke in her a conviction that her life must have some special purpose.

Her foster-father Arwîrac, whom the Romans call 'Caractacus', was confirmed at the assembly as commander of the feinidecht, the band of specially trained warriors chosen to serve the defence of all Britain. Truth be told, some of the British kings weren't so sure about that appointment and thought it a symptom of the Catuvellauni's overweening strength, which they feared the Romans might judge a provocation. Arwîrac knew that only united could the British stand against Roman might.

On the way east from the assembly, he delivered Gwladys to the druidic college at Cricklade, where she was to continue her studies in esoteric lore. There one day came a visitor: a grey-haired outlander, who spoke Latin with a strange exotic accent and whom Arwîrac had granted refuge amidst the sacred mire and mist of Glastonbury. His name was Joseph. Gwladys listened with fascination to his stories of his teacher in distant Judaea. It seemed to her there was much in this teacher's teaching — of the primacy of love, the forgiveness of sin, the promise of resurrection — that complemented the wisdom of the druids and responded to what had awoken in her at the Buckstone. Soon enough she gave her consent and a teenage princess became the first of all Britons to be baptised as a Christian.

In AD 43 the Romans came: four legions, fifty-thousand men, commanded by Aulus Plautius. The brothers Gwythr and Arwîrac led the coalition of tribes that tried to turn them back. For all the valour of the British warriors, for all the battle feats of the feini dancing along their chariot poles, the legions seemed unstoppable. After defeat at Porchester, Gwythr sued for peace and Plautius promised him a kingdom under Roman protection. In homage to the Emperor Claudius, Gwythr took the forenames 'Tiberius Claudius', and so by Roman custom his daughter Gwladys acquired the name 'Claudia'. Arwîrac was furious his brother had sold out. He rallied the remaining British troops and they fought so fiercely that they halted the Roman advance —

till the Emperor came to Britain with reinforcements, including elephants and artillery, and drove Arwîrac back to Winchester.

The siege dragged on for days. At last the Romans parleyed with Arwîrac via the silver tongue of Rufus Pudens, Plautius's aide-de-camp, a cultured young man who'd learnt the British tongue. Now, Claudius was a shrewder fellow than some thought; when he met Arwîrac face to face he saw how the other chieftains respected him; he saw that this was a man among men, whom Rome needed to keep the peace in this new province of the empire. Arwîrac, for his part, saw that what he'd feared had happened: that the Britons were divided and each of their kings was jockeying for advantage with the new power in the land. He perceived too that Pudens and Plautius were men of integrity. So a treaty was agreed: Gwythr to be king over the eastern tribes, with a new capital at Chichester; Arwîrac to be king over the tribes to the west, based in Gloucester; both subject to Plautius as governor; the treaty to be sealed by Arwîrac marrying the Emperor's own daughter, Genvissa.

Arwîrac was enchanted by Genvissa's dark Latin beauty. He, who for long years had been a roving war leader without wife or home, fell so deeply in love that he set upon making Gloucester, his capital in the land of the Dobunni, a city worthy of his Roman queen. In the palace the Romans built him there, Arwîrac and Genvissa were wed. Imagine the scene: the Roman officers gleaming in their brass and iron; the British chieftains and ladies with their plaid cloaks and long flowing hair, with torcs of gold encircling their throats and bands of gold round their arms.

It was on that happy day that young Gwladys met Rufus Pudens, the Governor's aide-de-camp. She was captivated by his charm and his learning: a man who could converse with her in her native tongue as well as in Latin and Greek, and was acquainted in Rome with such literati as Martial, whose verse she knew well. In Gwladys, Rufus found a young woman whose mind was bubbling from her studies and whose beauty was radiant with the faith in her heart. He fell in love with her and at the same time, as if it were a seamless part of the same thing, he was drawn to the Christ's teaching of which she spoke.

In the mingling of Romans and Britons in Gloucester, they had many opportunities to meet, for Aulus Plautius proved a humane governor who sought to respect the needs and ways of the native population so they might welcome what Rome had to offer.

But always things change. At the end of his tour of duty Plautius was recalled to Rome, and Rufus had to go with him. The evening before he left Gloucester, Rufus walked with Gwladys to the high ground of Hempsted, where they found a secluded spot to watch the sun set into the Dean hills beyond the river marking the Roman protectorate's boundary.

'Will you marry me, Gwladys, and come with me to Rome so we may live out our lives together and raise children wise in the ways of God?'

With all her heart as a woman, Gwladys wanted to say yes, to go with this sweet man, to bear his children, to live in the great city and meet its poets and philosophers, but she felt too the tug of loyalty to her foster-father and her people. 'I love you, Rufus. I hesitate only because I believe it is God's will that knowledge of the Christ should spread throughout this land, and that I may have a part to play in that purpose.'

As she spoke, the figure of a woman appeared, robed in white and walking up the hill from the Severn. Her face when she looked at them seemed to express all the sorrow and kindness in the world. She walked on along the slope, and then vanished. At that very spot a spring was bubbling from the turf. To Gwladys this vision and spring seemed a sign she must stay to serve God's will in Britain.

'Then', said Rufus, 'will you baptise me right here with water from this spring, so that though we may not share our lives together we yet may share the same faith.'

Under the new governor, Publius Ostorius Scapula, things changed in Britain. The Romans began to exploit the right of military might – to extort taxes, to take land, to rape women, to murder the druids, who they knew were the life blood of the Britons' collective identity. Scapula would not listen to Arwîrac's complaints. Arwîrac realised that in the fortress of Gloucester he was sitting inside a trap of his own making. He realised he'd made a terrible mistake. While he still could, he fled the city, with his wife and foster-daughter and all his household. He sent word to his old comrades of the feinidecht. From throughout Dobunni territory and further afield they slipped across the Severn to rendezvous with him in the Forest of Dean.

There he sought the chieftains of the unconquered Silures. 'I have learnt the truth about the Romans. Though there be honourable men among them, Rome's lust for power overrides the character of individual men. Rome will not stop till it has conquered all this island and made us all its slaves.'

The Silures hesitated – until their scouts reported Roman troops assembling on the Severn's east bank at Frampton where it was possible to cross at low tide. The Romans had spies too. They knew Arwîrac's location in the Forest. By crossing from Frampton, they could reach him quicker than they could via Gloucester.

The Silurian warriors who rushed to defend the west shore were hugely outnumbered. Their druids chanted to Sabrina, the lady of the river. The low tide had exposed mile-wide sand flats across that part of the river called 'the Noose'. In disciplined ranks, units of Roman cavalry and infantry, and elephants too, waded the narrow channel beside the east bank and marched across the wet sand. The warriors facing them, both men and women, cavorted and yelled and bared their bottoms. The druids shrieked their prayers to Sabrina. All that separated the front rank of legionaries from the enemy was another narrow channel. Javelins ready, they began to wade across.

Suddenly, faster than the Romans imagined possible, the flood tide came spilling up that channel. Sabrina had heard the druids' prayers! The front ranks splashed and stumbled back, colliding with the ranks behind. Water washed right across the rocks at the foot of Hock Cliff, where the river sharply turns, and back down the eastern channel, behind the Romans on the flats, to meet the tide flooding up that side too. The Noose was knotted. The troops were now encircled by deeper water than they'd bargained for. The cornicines sounded the retreat. Centurions yelled to keep their units in order. Already little streams were cutting across the sand between the two channels, braiding the flats into a lattice of islands and water. Stumbling and skidding in their armour, the soldiers began to panic. The horses neighed and stamped. The elephants trumpeted. Then there came a roar, louder every second, and a frothing, bristling wall of water came rushing upstream – the tidal bore – in which some thought they glimpsed a wild-haired woman riding a chariot drawn by dolphins. The bore knocked down the legionaries like bowling pins, struck the horsemen broadside. The units still on the bank could only watch helpless as it swept their comrades, even the elephants, beneath its unstoppable power.

After that the Silures were persuaded that the gods were on their side and that Arwîrac was right about the Romans' intentions. Spearheaded by his feini, they raided deep into Dobunni territory, torching the farms of those who collaborated with the Romans. Scapula brought together his legions and drove Arwîrac and the Silures back across the Severn. This time the river didn't stop the Romans. They hounded Arwîrac deep into the mountains. The hill tribes rose to Arwîrac's cause. He harried the legions in guerrilla style, always dodging back into the hills, retreating gradually northwards. Through all the hardships of moorland and wood, his Roman wife Genvissa and his foster-daughter Gwladys stayed loyally by his side.

What happened next is well known. The pitched battle in which the Romans had victory. The capture of Arwîrac's family. His escape north to seek refuge among the Brigantes. His betrayal into Roman hands. So it came about that Arwîrac was taken to Rome, and with him all his family and chief allies and lieutenants. Gwladys's dream of spreading Christ's teaching of love in Britain lay in ruins. To the city she could have come to as a bride she was brought as a captive in chains.

Under the hot Italian sun, along a paved road between massive stone buildings, through the yelling, staring mob, Scapula paraded his captives, Gwladys among them and Genvissa too, the Emperor's own daughter, now an enemy of Rome, both weeping in fear. Rufus Pudens was there among the Roman officers, horrified to see his beloved Gwladys stumbling in chains before the howling mob; horrified to think of the executioner's hands around her slender neck.

Last in line came Arwîrac, erect and proud in spite of his chains. They forced him to his knees before the dais where Claudius sat in his glory. And the British King said, 'As I look upon your great city, O Caesar, and see the splendour of its houses, I wonder why you, who have so many and such fine possessions, should covet us our poor tents. If I had enjoyed better luck in the turn of events, my rank and lineage would suffice for you to welcome me as friend, not captive. I had warriors, horses, weapons. Are you surprised I'm sorry to lose them? If you must lord it over all the world, O Caesar, do you expect that everyone else must welcome enslavement?'

Claudius was stirred by this speech. He made a gesture to the black-hooded man beside him. Gwladys fervently whispered to her God. The mob roared. The burly executioner stepped down beside Arwîrac. The mob held its breath. The executioner struck off the Briton's chains. Claudius gazed left and right to the silent crowd. Caesar has power over life and death. This time he chooses life.

Off came the chains of all Arwîrac's family. As soon as Gwladys was freed she fell weeping into the arms of Rufus.

'Do you love me still?' she cried.

'I love you as I love God: with all my heart.'

So in the capital of the world Gwladys and Rufus were reunited. Before law and God they became husband and wife. Arwîrac and Genvissa dwelt with them in their fine house in Rome, which became known as the 'Britannic Palace' and as a meeting place for Christians in the city. The new faith was tolerated so long as Claudius lived.

But then Claudius was murdered and Nero became Caesar and the time of tribulation began. The house of Rufus and Gwladys became a refuge for the persecuted, thanks to Rufus's connection with Aulus Plautius, the old war hero. In those years the apostle Paul came to Rome, and he too was a guest in the Britannic Palace. Long and convoluted were his conversations with Gwladys and Arwîrac, comparing Christian and druidic teaching. Paul was thrilled the gospel had reached so remote a land as Britain, and intrigued by the druids' notion of the three-fold nature of the divine. Arwîrac, for his part, pondered the way of war that he had lived, that had seemed so right, and yet had brought only disaster and defeat.

'The way of Christ is the way of peace,' Gwladys said. 'It's a wisdom that transcends the wisdom of the world.'

But how can you follow the way of peace when your land and people are stamped beneath an invader's feet? The news from Britain was getting worse. Nero hated the druids as he did the Jews and Christians, because they wouldn't acknowledge him as divine. In AD 57 he sent his hardman Gaius Suetonius Paulinus to be governor. You know what came next: the slaughter of druids in Anglesey, Boudicca's rebellion, the burning of London, all the killing that ensued. The situation got so desperate that at last the Romans allowed Arwîrac to return to Britain, to be king again in Gloucester and do what he could to make peace.

A few years later Paul went there too, his last missionary journey, to the uttermost west. In Gloucester he argued theology once more with Arwîrac and preached in the forum where the city's four main streets join. He crossed the Severn into country not yet annexed by Rome, hoping to meet druids and debate with them as he'd done with the philosophers in Athens. But so many of the druids had been killed, and those who remained lived in hiding in the woods.

When Paul returned to Rome, he met his death by Nero's command in the same terrible purge that took the life of Rufus Pudens. Arwîrac lived on till AD 74. He was buried in Gloucester and his son and grandson became kings after him. His great-grandson Lucius, crowned king by the druids, asked the Pope to send preachers to teach the Christian faith throughout Britain. At Winchester, Lucius proclaimed his faith in Christ and received baptism, as did many of his people. In Gloucester he built a church on the site of what is now St Mary de Lode and there was buried when he died. Some say it was the first church built in Britain, though surely that honour must be Glastonbury's.

Gwladys – now known as 'Claudia Rufina' – never returned to her homeland. In Rome her house continued to be a haven for Christians in those fearful times. She lived to a great age. After the death of Simon Peter, her son Linus became the bishop of Rome.

Twenty

THE DEERHURST DRAGON

There were once many dragons in Britain, but as people became more numerous and spread to every corner of the land, the dragons became fewer, till you'd be lucky – or unlucky – to see one outside their last strongholds in the north and the west.

The last dragon in the kingdom of the Hwicce lurked in the wilds of Deerhurst. They say she was one of the very last dragons east of the Severn. Deerhurst, as the name suggests, was once a marshy, woody place frequented by wild beasts such as deer, which amply served the dragon's appetite. It was rare that anyone caught a glimpse of her, except at dusk when she'd take to the wing – whether for exercise or in hope of luring a mate from Wales – and her long spiky pinions might be seen silhouetted against the sunset.

But times were changing. Some monks established a mission on the bank of the Severn. No doubt their intention was to escape the distractions of society and test their souls against the wild, but one thing led to another, their little monastery became an abbey, and their wooden chapel a tall stone minster, where even kings were buried. The monks cultivated the land around the

abbey and other people settled nearby. To feed their multiplying children, the people gradually cleared more and more land of its trees and thickets so they could till the soil and graze their cattle.

Before long, most of the deer were gone. The dragon, whose lair was hidden in the last patch of wild country, took to preying on cattle. In truth, they were easier to catch than fleet-footed deer and carried more meat. The cattle's owners, whether monk or churl, were never happy to lose one, but the further they let their animals wander in search of pasture, the greater was the risk that, with a swirling of fangs and talons and wings, the dragon would nab one. She also liked to wallow in the pools among the willows, which did no harm to the frogs and water voles, but when thirsty cowherds drank the water they'd sometimes sicken. People those days knew nothing of bacteria; they said the dragon had poisoned them.

At last there was such grievance against the dragon that the Abbot drew up a petition of complaint. All who could write their name signed it, and the rest applied an inky thumbprint, and the petition was sent to the King at Winchcombe. While they waited, the dragon disappeared from the evening sky as if she knew that trouble was brewing. Some weeks later a thane arrived on horseback, with a splendid brooch on his breast to prove he represented the King.

The thane took out a roll of parchment. Everyone gathered in the abbey yard, even the women and children, to hear the proclamation:

'That this hundred of Deerhurst be relieved of the gluttonous and pestilential wyrm sent by the Devil to test the faith and fortitude of our subjects, we hereby decree that whosoever shall slay this wyrm, and present its head as proof of the deed, shall be granted in perpetuity the estate of land commonly known as Walton Hill.'

There was an awkward silence. There was a shifting about and an avoiding of each other's gaze. No doubt they'd expected a troop of mailed housecarls armed to the teeth. Instead the King had thrown the problem back on their own resources. You might say it was an early instance of the Big Society. And Walton Hill was the last parcel of land anyone would want: the very nest of bog, bramble and gnats where the dragon was laired.

But there was among them a poor Saxon villein who dreamt of making a better life for himself, and the chance of marrying a good woman and raising children of his own, and was ready to stake his life for that dream. His name was John Smith

'I will hazard this challenge,' he said. 'But I be a poor man. I do ask of this rich abbey two things to aid me.

With a collective sigh of relief that someone else had offered, everyone turned expectantly to the Abbot.

'Tell us what you need,' said the Abbot warily. He reckoned that a poor man would take whatever he could get.

'An axe,' said John, 'and a barrel of milk of a size as a strong man can lug on his back.

'Axe and milk you shall have. But if you return with neither milk nor dragon's head, we shall know you for a thief and you will forfeit one hand. Come back without the axe and you'll forfeit the other hand too.'

With an axe in his hand and a barrel of milk strapped heavy on his back, John Smith entered the marshy thickets below Walton Hill. It was a hot summer day; the flies buzzed round his face, the brambles and briars tore at his limbs, and he could see no more than a few yards through the greenery. The dragon might be in the bushes right beside him and he'd never know till she struck.

At last he found what he wanted: an open space of sun-dried mud beside a pool, hedged by willows and thorny undergrowth. He put down the barrel and lopped off its top with the axe; then he hid in the thorns, axe in hands, and waited. His back ached from carrying such a weight. Flies tormented him and whirled above the open barrel. How long would he have to wait? Was the dragon even at home, or had she flown west to Wales? Maybe she was here already, hiding, watching the bait. Dragons are cunning beasts, John knew. They've got more of a mind than an animal has a right to. That's why they had no place in a civilised land. He waited so long that the sun began to descend. You wouldn't want to get stuck out here at night. But no way could he carry back the milk now he'd cut off the top of the barrel; and if he returned without the milk, that hard-faced abbot would cut off his hand.

There came a sound like the slithery clanking of oiled chain mail. From across the pool a long scaly snout appeared. The eyes were sunken pools of darkness. A beetroot tongue scented the air. The long neck, the snaky body and taloned limbs, the folded-back wings and long tapering tail oozed slowly from the thorns. Every inch of her was armoured with iron-hard scales, small and densely packed on her topside, broader on the belly, grey-green in hue as if she were a part of the woods and the earth. She circled the barrel of milk, closer and closer, so her body became a spiral. Her head reared up and she peered down into the barrel. Her tongue dipped in to taste what was there.

The dragon knew that men had little love for her kind. She knew her own power and that they had reason to fear her. She knew that in some times and places dragons have been honoured like gods, and their goodwill sought with offerings. A barrel of milk was not a prize bull, or a virgin girl, or a hoard of gold, but the people in these parts were humble folk; for them, perhaps, a barrel of milk might seem a lordly sacrifice. And it's true that, like cats and snakes, dragons do have a liking for milk.

Yet, she was wary. How else would she have lived to such an age? And there was more at stake than her own life. With a slither of scaly skin she unfurled her wings. Two strong beats took her above the trees to soar in a circle round the muddy clearing and peer down through the leaves for the tell-tale sparkle of helmet or spear. John Smith clutched his axe to his chest and held so still he didn't breathe.

As suddenly, the dragon swooped back to the barrel. She arched her sinuous neck, dipped in her snout, and began to drink. Lovely warm milk, with a cheesy flavour after its hours in the sun. She drank and drank till the barrel was empty and her stomach and gizzard were full. She felt so bloated that she rolled on her back and basked in the sun, ruffling the big scales on her belly to let the air at her skin.

Now or never! Out leapt John Smith with his axe. He picked a spot where creamy skin showed between the ruffled scales, and whacked the blade down. Blood spurted and splattered. The dragon's scream blew back the willow branches like a gale. The man pulled back the axe to strike again. But the belly scales snapped closed. The dragon twisted to her feet. Her wings rushed open and knocked him headlong into the pool. She flapped to get airborne, screamed again at the pain, too fierce to let her fly, and dragged herself away through the trees.

By the time John had clambered from the water she was gone. But she'd left a trail of thick dark blood. Through the labyrinth of thorns, trees, marshes, pools he followed her, up and down, around and back, till the trail of blood led up a steep scarp, to woodland dry underfoot, shady and cool, and then uphill again, a thicketed tump, steep on every side.

On the top of that tump he ran her to ground. Curled up in a nest of hawthorn, bramble and burdock, the dragon looked smaller than she had stretching in the sun or circling in the sky. She wasn't alone. Peeping from her coils was her little one. Its scales all shiny and new, its wings mere buds on its back, it peered up at John Smith with liquid big eyes. The wounded mother too looked up at him; in her deep dark eyes were all the memories, all the glory and the sadness, she'd seen. She was weak from the blood she'd lost. She could not fight or flee. She could not abandon her infant.

The scales on her neck were thick and tough. It took eight blows to sever her head. Thus John Smith's quest was won, but the task was not yet finished. He wasn't a heartless man; it pained him to see how the little one nuzzled the mother's headless carcass. But he knew there's no place for dragons in civilised country. He needed this land for himself and his children.

The baby dragon's scales were thin and soft. One blow of the axe did the job. John tied the two heads together with cord and strung them from his shoulders for the journey back. The people of Deerhurst cheered when they saw the deed was done – but they were alarmed to see a second dragon's head.

'A whole nest of them breeding up there!'

John Smith assured them there were no more. 'The sire must a-come from Wales.'

The Abbot hung the heads behind the minster's altar, as an offering to God in thanks for Deerhurst's deliverance from the Devil's minions. They soon stank too much to stay there, so he had a mason sculpt two dragons' heads of stone to replace them.

John Smith the dragon-killer was granted the estate promised by the King. By his own hands he cleared the trees and thickets. He grew fields of turnips and carrots and grazed a herd of cattle. He gained a wife and then sons and daughters to help him. So the land changed. Only in a few nooks below the scarp do the marshes and thickets remain. The two stone dragon heads still adorn the chancel of St Peter's in Deerhurst. And roundabout Walton Hill, they say, there's still a farmer by the name of Smith and on his land a knoll known as Dragon's Tump.

Twenty-one

THE LADY OF THE MIST

All there is to see of Kempsford Castle today is a walled terrace along the riverside rampart and at one end a mullioned window looking blindly upon the water. But on moonlit nights, it's said, a ghostly figure appears above the mist, in a thin grey gown, her face pale, her arms folded across her breast, her hair snaking in the air. It is the ghost of Lady Maud de Chaworth, who once owned this castle.

Maud inherited the place as a child when her father died. Here in her teens she was courted by young Henry Plantagenet. They would sit in the sun on the ramparts to watch the ducks squabbling on the Thames, and they'd sneak down to be alone together in the secret room that could be reached only from the riverbank. They married young and she bore him seven children, but a long life of wedded bliss was not to be theirs.

They lived in the time of Edward II, an unwilling king who entrusted power to a succession of self-serving favourites. Maud was half-sister to Hugh le Despenser, the last to win that role from the King. Her husband was brother to Thomas, Earl of Lancaster, who lost his life opposing Despenser's regime. Upon his execution the vast estates of Lancaster were forfeit to the Crown, but Henry was their rightful heir. In 1326, when Queen Isabella and her adulterous consort Roger Mortimer invaded to seize England from its king, and Edward raised his banner in Gloucester, it was Henry who led the desertion of English earls to Isabella's side.

When Henry took troops into Wales in pursuit of the fleeing King and Despenser, he left one of his knights at Kempsford for Maud's protection. Sir Basil Fitzwarren would seem a harmless, callow young fellow to a lady of Maud's rank and maturity, yet she was a beautiful woman and he took a gallant shine to her.

'You must be lonely, my lady, your husband away all these weeks,' he would sally. 'Perhaps my lady would enjoy a turn upon the ramparts while the sunset is so fine.'

Maud gave him no more attention than courtesy required. If her heart was torn by the loyalty she felt to her king and her brother, there remained between her and her husband a love beyond words or the world's troubles. When Basil saw how she spurned his advances, he tried them no more; yet surreptitiously he watched her coming and going about the manor and took what pleasure his eyes could grant.

In open country near Neath, Henry Plantagenet ran King Edward to ground – along with Despenser and a few loyal men-at-arms. Henry escorted the King to Kempsford, where Lady Maud received him with all honour as their sovereign lord. When news came from Hereford that a court had put Despenser to death by unspeakable means, both Edward and Maud retched and wept, for each had loved him in their way.

'Hugh was a ruthless man, it's true,' Maud cried to her husband, 'but why must people be so horrible to each other?'

'What this country needs is firm, ordered government,' Henry said.

And Sir Basil Fitzwarren watched how Maud wept on her husband's shoulder and how he held her tight in his arms, and Basil wished those arms were his.

From Kempsford, Henry took the King to Kenilworth Castle and continued to treat him with due respect, while Mortimer and the Queen took steps to compel his abdication in favour of fourteen-year-old Prince Edward. The more Henry saw of Mortimer's conduct as co-regent, the more he realised that the man was as grasping and ambitious as Despenser. Not Henry only. A conspiracy was afoot, led by the brothers Thomas and Stephen Dunheved, to free the deposed king. Mortimer and Isabella worried that Edward might not be as secure as they'd like in Henry Plantagenet's hands. They had Henry relinquish him to Thomas de Berkeley, who conveyed him to his own castle at Berkeley.

The usurpers could not openly take Edward's life, for in the Church's eyes he was anointed by God. Subtlety was needed. Edward's gaolers in Berkeley Castle hacked off his handsome curly locks; they fed him foul food; they kept him in a room with an open shaft from which came the noxious stink of carrion rotting in the dungeon beneath, where a hideous toad had grown huge feeding on the carcasses of prisoners and animals. It was terrible for a man used to luxury and privilege to be reduced to such straits. Edward's groans of self-pity could be heard through the castle, including by the workmen Lord Berkeley had brought in to repair damage done by Despenser's troops a year before. What the gaolers didn't know was that these workmen had been infiltrated by agents of the Dunheveds. Members of the conspiracy were camped nearby in the wilds of Berkeley Heath and Michael Wood. Men-at-arms had mustered from across the Cotswolds in hopes of freeing Edward. Lady Maud knew about them. Some had stayed at Kempsford en route to the Vale.

Edward sickened in his squalid confinement, but did not die. His constitution was stronger than his gaolers had hoped. One day the servant who attended him whispered, 'Sire, I've heard them planning. They have orders to kill you ... by ... by ...'

'For God's sake, man, tell me!'

'To do it by a method that will leave no mark on Your Highness's body.'

That night Edward suffered nightmares of an agonising death. His blood-curdling screams rang loud enough to be heard out on Berkeley Heath. Secret messages passed to and fro. The Dunheved men knew they had to act. They tramped by night through the marshes to the castle walls. A man who'd been smuggled in with the workmen opened the postern gate. Suddenly there was an uproar of battle within the walls. The intruders were even inside the keep, stamping up the steps to Edward's room.

The confusion of that night hangs down like a veil through history. Lord Berkeley was absent from the castle. He was strangely slow to act, first requesting permission from the Queen before he hunted down the fleeing raiders. Some were caught. Others got away. In ones and twos, hungry and exhausted, fugitives arrived at Kempsford Castle. Maud fed them, gave them a bed for the night, saw them across the Thames. Sir Basil Fitzwarren asked no questions. All he cared about was the sight of Maud's fair face animated by her kindness and concern.

With two companions came one who seemed a broken man – malnourished, dressed in rags, bristly stubble on his pate and chin. He was too weak to flee further. In dead of night, while the household slept, Maud sent the two companions across the river, but led the other man down hidden stairs to the riverbank and the room beneath the rampart. In the wee hours each night she wrapped a cloak around her shift and slipped barefoot down the secret stairs with food and drink for her secret guest.

In November 1327, it was made known that Edward of Caernarvon, formerly king of England, had died 'of natural causes' in Berkeley Castle. His body was embalmed not by a court physician but by a local woman, who after doing the job was escorted to the Queen in Worcester – with Edward's heart in a silver casket – and then disappeared. The corpse was sealed in a lead coffin. But who would bury the enemy of the She-Wolf and her lover who now lorded it over England? The abbeys of Bristol, Malmesbury and Kingswood said no. It was St Peter's Abbey, Gloucester that took him. They say that stags came from the woods to draw the royal coffin, and that the common folk lined the roads in droves to bid their king farewell, and that wherever the cortège paused they planted an oak to mark the spot. In Gloucester's minster the coffin was laid to rest in a splendid tomb.

Back in Kempsford, Basil was lying sleepless in bed one night when he heard soft footsteps in the passageway. From his room he crept, to glimpse Lady Maud in nightgown and cloak as she passed through a shaft of moonlight from a loophole. Curious why she was carrying a tray of food, he stole after her. Down a stairway he hadn't known existed he followed her, to the riverbank, and saw her enter the secret room below the rampart. He heard a man's voice. She had a lover down there! The two-faced harlot! Before dawn Basil was riding north to report to his lord Henry, the newly made Earl of Lancaster.

When Henry heard what Basil had to tell, he was too furious to think. That Maud should take a lover in the very trysting place of their youth! He rode to Kempsford post-haste. He arrived in the dead of night, ran down the secret stairs to the riverbank and the door of the secret room. He had no eyes for the moonlight shining through the willows, or the ghostly radiance it gave to the mist rising from the water and coiling among the reeds. The door opened as he arrived: before him was a gaunt-faced man with short bristly hair. With one blow he threw the man against a table, sending dishes and jugs smashing on the floor. There stood Maud in her shift and cloak. With all the strength of his rage Henry seized her. The cloak fell from her shoulders as he dragged her outside. Oblivious of her cries, he hurled her in the Thames.

The felled man scrabbled to his feet. 'I tell you, Henry, your wife is true. She has but given sanctuary to a ruined man.'

Henry knew that voice. He stared at the man in astonishment. Then his thoughts turned to Maud. He could hear her thrashing and gasping in the water, but couldn't see her through the mist, and the current was carrying her away. He crashed along the bank, between the jungly trunks of the willows, startling waterbirds from sleep. He struggled on and on till exhaustion from the long ride overcame him.

In the morning Maud's body was found a mile downstream. The guest in the secret room was gone, his dinner uneaten. Henry was stricken with grief and guilt. Not long after that tragic night his eyesight began to fail. In a few years he was blind; he considered it God's judgement on his crime. Before his sight left him, he played his part in Edward III's coup to seize power from Mortimer and the Queen. Afterwards Henry returned to Kempsford, where he'd once known happiness with Maud, and gave his declining years to God. He rebuilt the chancel of the church as an act of penitence in honour of his late wife. In a sculpted tomb in that chancel was buried Sir Basil Fitzwarren, who too undertook penitence and lived the rest of his days as a monk.

Yet another man who'd devoted himself to the religious life, garbed in a beggar's rags, wandered the highways and byways of Europe till at last he came to Lombardy. In a remote corner of the Apennines, this man found refuge for his body and soul at the Hermitage of St Alberto di Butrio. In one of its churches is a tomb, now empty, that local legend says was the burial place of an English king who lived out his days in this hermitage.

On moonlit nights, even today in Kempsford, a pale lady will appear above the mist and drift along the riverside terrace known as 'Lady Maud's Walk'. If you listen carefully you may hear her singing, in a thin voice like the wind, a lament of the happy days of her youth, when her dashing husband loved her and all the joy you might hope for in life yet seemed possible.

Twenty-two

POOR JIM AND
DEAD JIM

Jim Wilcox was a Stroud weaver, a skilled one and proud of it. But the price of wool was up, the price of cloth was down, they could make it for half the cost in Yorkshire, and always the mill owners would take those tough decisions – to preserve their income and let the workers take the hit, whether it was longer hours for less pay, or less regular work, or no work at all. Jim lost his job and it was as well he had no dependants, since he could find no other. Some might say he was too proud, or too set in his ways, but the fact of the matter was he had no work, no money, and nowhere to live except up the hill in the Union Workhouse. With the aged, the orphans, the mentally impaired, and fellow castoffs of the wool industry, he was set digging the earth for potatoes and carrots. Can you judge him if he didn't put his back into it? He was a weaver, a good one, and he hated this paupers' slavery, and the dank prison of a building, and his ceaseless hunger for a stouter ration of food.

Jim's relatives on his dear departed mother's side were not badly off, but they were as sympathetic as the mill owners towards his well-being. Once he was in the workhouse, they were yet less inclined to acknowledge any connection. They never lifted a finger to help him in his time of need, until one day Mrs Sybil Miles, Jim's second cousin once removed, heard a knock at the door of her nice cottage in Painswick. It was a letter from the Master of Stroud Union Workhouse, advising her that Mr James Wilcox, to whom she was presumed next of kin, was deceased, and asking whether the family would pay for the funeral or the body was to be buried by the parish.

In a bit of a flap, Mrs Miles consulted the rest of the family. All agreed that it would reflect badly on them if one of theirs should be dumped in a pauper's grave. So they clubbed together to provide a swanky funeral in Painswick. The church was booked, the coffin was carpentered, the grave was dug, the parson wrote his sermon, a banquet was prepared, and on the appointed day Jim's relatives, decked in black like a flock of rooks, gathered in the cottage of Mrs Miles.

Charlie Harris, a friend of the family, drove the coffin on a wagon down to Stroud and up Bisley Road to the tall, slab-sided edifice of the workhouse. Four inmates carried the body from the mortuary. Charlie took one solemn look – and declared, 'That's not Jim Wilcox!'

'It do be he,' the paupers said.

'No, it's not. I've known Jim since he were a lad.'

The Master arrived just then on the scene. 'I assure you most certainly that this is Jim Wilcox.'

Right at that moment Jim's face appeared at a grimy window of the workhouse. He waved a greeting at Charlie.

'That's Jim there!'

The Master shook his head in bafflement and bustled off to check the paperwork. It turned out that not one but two paupers by the name of James Wilcox were – or had been – inmates of the workhouse.

'I am very sorry for this misapprehension,' said the Master.

'It's all right being sorry,' said Charlie, 'but it's too late: the grave, the funeral, the banquet have all been arranged; the relatives are waiting.'

'What do you expect me to do if the man insists on being alive?'

'There's only one thing for it: I'll have to take Jim to his funeral. They won't believe me otherwise that he ain't dead.'

So Jim put on what he had left of his Sunday best and sat in the coffin on Charlie's wagon as they drove off up to Painswick. After weeks in the workhouse and grubbing in its vegetable plots, he looked about with keen pleasure at the lovely views into the valley, till at last the tall spire of Painswick Church hove in sight.

'Why do the bells toll so solemn-like?' he asked.

'Have you forgotten why we've come? They're tolling for your funeral.'

At the cottage Mrs Miles came to the door. Her powdered face bore an expression of studied sorrow.

'Hello, Auntie!' cried Jim from the coffin.

Her mouth dropped open – and she screamed and fled inside, slamming the door behind her. Murmurs of consternation from within. Tentatively the door reopened and the black-robed relatives filed out and regarded Jim with an air of reproach. They began to debate what should be done – about the grave, the parson, the banquet, the mourners who'd soon be arriving.

'If we stopped those bells ringing, it would be a start,' said Charlie, and hurried into the church, where the sexton was hauling away at the ropes. 'Stop the bells! He's not dead!'

'What's that?' mouthed the sexton, who couldn't hear a word above the bells' solemn slow knell.

Charlie grabbed the ropes to try to stop them. The outraged sexton resisted. The solemn slow knell became a cacophony.

Charlie wouldn't give up. The sexton started throwing punches, till some mourners appeared and dragged the men apart.

But Charlie had the bit between his teeth. 'The parson needs to be told!' Out he ran, through the phalanx of yews, to find the parson beside the freshly dug grave, prayer book clasped to his belly, and looking startled by the tuneless noise from the tower.

'It's all right, Reverend,' Charlie gasped. 'He ain't dead.'

'What on earth do you mean?'

'Jim's not dead.'

'But he died and therefore he must be dead. Only our Lord hath risen from the tomb. Mr Wilcox hasn't yet even been put in his grave.'

Charlie took a deep breath. 'You best come with me, Reverend.'

Back at Mrs Miles's, most of the relatives had departed, rather put out that they'd come here on false pretences and had forked out to pay for the funeral. The banquet was there still, and so was Jim, tucking in for all he was worth to satisfy his hunger.

'Upon my soul!' cried the vicar. 'How small was my faith! Seeing not, I believed not, but now that I see I do believe that he liveth!'

And now that Jim lived Mrs Sybil Miles was only too keen to see the back of him. So back to the workhouse Charlie took him. It was grim after his day out to be back inside those cold damp walls with the other discards of society, and back to gruel and bread and ten hours a day of heavy work in the vegetable plots. No doubt it was because of his brief heady experience of luxury, and being the centre of attention, that Jim felt more than usually irked when the Master shouted at him to put his back into the work.

'I won't do it at all if you yell at me.'

'How dare you speak to me in such a manner!' cried the Master.

'I'm a damn good weaver and I know what my labour's worth.'

The other paupers were listening and leering to see what the Master would do. The Master knew well that the poor must be kept in their place, or where would we all be? He called for the porter and they put Jim alone in the mortuary with no food all day. 'That'll take him down a peg,' the Master reckoned.

Jim wasn't quite alone, because in the same room, wrapped in a shroud in a coffin, lay the corpse of the other Jim Wilcox, waiting to be taken across to the cemetery and down Pauper's Path to an unmarked grave. It was fearfully cold in the mortuary. Poor Jim sat shivering in the corner, trying not to think about the coffin and its occupant. As the light from the window faded, he got colder and hungrier and more and more fearful to be spending the night with a corpse. He banged on the door and yelled to be let out. But no one came. The cold and hunger and fear made him angry. The anger sparked an idea. He took a deep breath to bolster his nerve and lifted the corpse from its coffin and sat it in the corner. He swopped his workhouse jacket for its shroud, wrapped the shroud round himself, and lay down in the coffin. He'd got used to being in a coffin on the way to his funeral, so it wasn't too bad, and after a time he felt snug and warm enough in there to sleep.

As the morning light glowed through the window, and Jim drifted awake, he heard the key turning in the lock. He kept very still in the coffin and waited. The Master came in with a tray of bread and water; in the dim grey light he could make out Jim Wilcox sitting asleep in the corner.

'Here's your breakfast then,' he said in a loud voice to wake the rascal.

The figure in the corner did not stir.

'Don't you want your breakfast?' the Master bellowed.

The corpse made no reply.

Jim, lying shrouded in the coffin, allowed a nice pause, then jerked bolt upright. 'If he don't want it, then I'll have it.'

The Master shrieked and stared, his lips working at the air, and passed out on the cold stone floor.

The mortuary door was open – Jim could have fled his confinement right then, and fled the workhouse too; but, the thing is, although the workhouse might seem like a prison, in truth it was not. Its inmates were only there because they'd nowhere else to go. Poor Jim reclaimed his jacket and wrapped dead Jim in the shroud and heaved him back into the coffin. Then he went to find Matron to tell her that the Master seemed to be feeling unwell.

Twenty-three

THE KING'S REVENGE

When the hostilities of the Civil War had ceased and King Charles had fallen into the power of his rebel Parliament, the leaders of the revolution parleyed with him to decide how England would be governed. But the King was tricky. Though conclusively defeated, he refused to compromise his belief in the divine right of his authority. In November 1647 he escaped to the Isle of Wight and there conducted secret negotiations with the Scots. A Scottish army invaded from the north and Royalist uprisings broke out in parts of England and Wales. In his relentless way – unbeatable in battle – Cromwell soon dealt with all that. Now his attitude towards the King hardened. He became convinced there could be no security from further Royalist rebellion so long as the King remained alive. With his allies in the army and the radical party in Parliament, he demanded the King be tried for high treason.

On so grave a matter the opinion of Parliament was divided. Among the moderate party was one Colonel Nathaniel Stephens, MP for Gloucestershire. He'd fought for Parliament throughout the war and was respected by everyone. In the

House of Commons he argued, 'What we ought to abhor is not the person or the institution of the King, but rather the excesses in his policy. I have no stomach for this stranger cure my right honourable friends have proposed – that we should do away with the King. We must exercise all our might and imagination to make with him a treaty by which his powers may be curbed and the rights and weal of all Englishmen may be respected.'

But the tide of history was running fast. A little before Christmas 1648, Colonel Stephens was with his family at his home, Chavenage House, near Tetbury, to celebrate that season of goodwill, when a party of horsemen clip-clopped into the yard. The footman showed into the hall a stern-faced man dressed all in black, save for his broad white collar. It was Henry Ireton, Cromwell's son-in-law and lieutenant, who was also related by marriage to Stephens.

'I'm here to ask you to come to London,' said Ireton. 'There's to be a vote to bring the King to trial. We need your vote and the regard in which other members hold you.'

Stephens looked into the flames crackling in the great fireplace. 'You know my views on this matter.'

'I do, and I was once of the same mind; but a man's mind may change with the course of events and upon cogitation. I believe that this "cure" is the right thing to do. It's the only thing that will bring stability and the need many feel for justice to be done.'

Suddenly a young woman burst into the hall – Abigail, the Colonel's daughter, who'd heard who the visitor was and why he was here. In her wide staring eyes burned tiny reflections of the fire.

'You mustn't go with him, Father! You mustn't have anything to do with such an unholy crime!'

'You speak out of turn,' said her brother, Robert. 'Mr Ireton speaks good sense. It will be an honourable thing, Father, to vote for this measure and bring the lasting peace that people so desperately desire.'

Abigail's eyes blazed yet wider, staring right through the men as if she were seeing some vision beyond the hall in which they stood. 'Please, Father, don't go! If you are implicated in the murder of the King, then you will surely sicken and die and the line of your descendants in this house will be extinguished.'

In the stunned silence the only sound was the crackling of the fire.

At last Robert found his voice: 'Abigail, you must not speak to your father so.'

'It's true! I know it!' She collapsed into sobs and the servants hustled her away to her room.

The three men repaired to the oak-panelled drawing room and debated the question through most of the night, until at last Ireton was prevailed upon to retire to the bedroom made ready for him. In the remaining hours of darkness Colonel Stephens slept badly, haunted by dreams of his daughter's staring eyes and her voice clamouring, 'Only God has the right to take a man's life – and most of all a king's!'

But the dogged logic of Ireton's argumentation had worn down his will. When he woke to the grey December dawn, he knew in his heart what he wanted to do – to stay here with his family and enjoy the blessed season of Christ's coming – and he knew in his mind what he had to do. Or at least he thought he did.

That morning, Stephens rode off with Henry Ireton and his escort of helmeted Ironsides – to London. It's believed he did vote for the King to be tried for treason against his own kingdom, but Stephens took no part in the court and his signature doesn't appear on the death warrant. The course of history turned. On 30 January 1649, King Charles was beheaded and England became a republic.

A few months later Colonel Stephens fell sick, as his daughter had prophesied. It was a lingering illness that kept him in bed for month after month, for year after year. Ten years went by and still he languished in his bed. A new king returned from across the sea. Not long after that, the Colonel's illness took a rapid turn for the worse. His relations and friends hastened to Chavenage. The yard was cluttered with their carriages as they gathered round his bed to say their farewells and pay their respects.

As the Colonel breathed his last breaths, another carriage, one gorgeously ornamented with gold and drawn by black horses, came silently up the drive. Soundlessly its door opened.

Then, before the astonished eyes of everyone kneeling or standing round the bed, the shade of Nathaniel Stephens rose from his
lifeless body and glided down the stairs, through the hall, through
the porch, and into the waiting carriage. The carriage door soundlessly closed. The driver lashed his whip, the horses began to pull
away, and everyone saw that the driver was a headless man, finely
dressed, wearing the blue velvet strap of the Garter round his left
calf and the star of the Garter on his left breast. He drove the carriage silently back down the drive. Upon reaching the gateway the
horses, carriage, driver and all vanished into a wall of flames.

It's said that every lord of Chavenage, when he dies, takes his departure in that same spectral conveyance. And in due course the rest of
Abigail's prophecy came true in some sense. The last descendant of
Nathaniel Stephens in the male line, Henry Stephens, died without issue in 1795. Chavenage was inherited by a cousin in a female
line, who quickly went insane, whereupon the house passed to a
niece, Alice, who was married to a Reverend Townshend of County
Cork. The Townshend Stephens, as the couple called themselves, lost
all their money trying to grapple with the devastating consequences
of the Irish Famine. They had to mortgage Chavenage. There was no
way they could repay the debt and so, in 1891, the house was sold
out of the Stephens family for good.

Twenty-four

THE PRICE OF A LAWYER'S SOUL

In the city of Bristol there was once a lawyer who had great wealth in gold and lands, in houses and livestock. There was a reason why he was so rich. In the business he conducted as both a merchant and what today we'd call a banker, he applied his mastery of the law's convoluted subtlety of meaning to screw people out of as much money as he could. He preyed especially on the poor and the gullible. He even evaded the payment of tithes to the Church, just as today a clever executive may dodge taxes by their knowledge of loopholes in the law.

This lawyer had one son, to whom he planned to leave all his fortune so the boy would be a great man in the kingdom.

'But you'll need education as well as capital, my lad.'

So he sent him to study with the priests – the best education to be had back then. From the priests the boy learnt his letters and languages and the skills of reason and rhetoric; but he learnt from them also something his father hadn't foreseen: he became godly and wise beyond his years.

'Next, my son, you'll need some training in law' – for the world was ruthless, as the lawyer knew better than anyone, and a man of means had to take care of his wealth.

The boy, in his bloom of godliness, said, 'I will not study such a subject that might jeopardise the state of my soul.'

His wish was to become an honest merchant, who bought and sold at fair prices the things people needed to live their lives. So he asked if he might be apprenticed to a certain merchant who was known for his honesty. To this his father agreed. By his truthfulness and courtesy the boy won the admiration of the merchant, who came to love the youth as if he were his own son.

Meanwhile the lawyer carried on swindling people, by every cunning means, to build up as big as possible the fortune he would leave to his heir when he died. That day, however, was destined to come sooner than he'd expected. An illness took hold in his intestine. Though his money could pay for the best doctors to attend him, it could not fight the disease. The tumours spread through his body. Soon the lawyer knew he was not long for this world.

In his fine mansion in Redcliffe Street he summoned to his bedside one after another of his business acquaintances, all great men of the city. He asked each of them in turn if they would be his executor. Each of them demurred. They knew by what means the lawyer had won his great fortune and were chary of accepting any public association with it.

There was only one person left to turn to. The lawyer sent for his son.

'I shall soon be gone from this life, my son. You are my sole heir; all my wealth will be yours. But I must ask you also to be the executor of my will.'

The youth, despite his tender years, had long guessed the character of his father's style of business. He said nothing.

His dying father understood the meaning of his silence and averted gaze. 'Time is short,' he croaked. 'I charge you to be my executor. Only if you do this will I give you my blessing as your father.'

The son loved his father, even if he hated the things his father had done. He was troubled by the thought that any soul might be imperilled for the sake of wealth that he would inherit.

'I will be your executor,' he said. 'But I charge you in return that on the fourteenth day after you pass from this life you shall appear to me, so I may know how your soul fares in the hereafter.'

The lawyer gave his pledge. That very night his condition worsened. The priest came to give him the sacrament and pray for God's mercy on his soul. Before sunrise he was dead.

His son gave him a magnificent funeral, with a battalion of mourners to mourn him, and gave lavish hospitality to everyone who came, rich and poor, those who'd known his father and those who had not. People rushed from all over the city to make the most of his largesse. Afterwards he employed a hundred priests to pray every day for his father's soul. To do all this, he spent the gold he'd inherited, and sold all his father's property in Bristol, save only the house in Redcliffe Street. In fourteen days all that money was spent.

On that fourteenth day, while the youth was kneeling in prayer, there came a cacophony of roaring and screams, a stench of brimstone and burning flesh, and he saw a vision of a naked man, chained by the neck, whose body was enveloped in bright golden flames and glowed like hot coals.

'Are you my father?'

'I am,' groaned the man. 'I suffer now the punishment for swindling so many people of what was rightly theirs. So shall I forever be punished unless all that I took by extortion or deceit is returned.'

'I'll see what I can do. Only give me your pledge that you'll appear to me again in another fourteen days.'

The father gave his pledge and vanished in a puff of smoke.

The youth still had his father's lands beyond the city, but he lacked any cash. So he went to his former master, the honest merchant, and asked him for a loan while he sought buyers for his lands.

'You'd have no need of a loan if you hadn't spent so extravagantly that great fortune you inherited!'

The youth desired not to speak of his father's infernal punishment. 'I have lands in plenty, sir, but it may take some time to realise from them the capital by which to repay the loan I urgently need.'

The merchant yet loved the youth, and his heart softened. 'Tell me how much your lands are worth.'

'In total about £1,000' – which back then was the equivalent of many millions today.

Out of his great regard for the boy, the merchant said, 'I will pay £2,000 to buy all your lands.'

With that money in hand, the lawyer's son had a proclamation made that whosoever his father had swindled out of any sum, large or small, should come and declare it and the debt would be satisfied in full. Come they did, hundreds of them, the youth paid them all, and in fourteen days all that huge sum of £2,000 was spent.

On that fourteenth day, while the youth knelt in prayer, his father appeared to him again as pledged; no longer in chains, no longer glowing like hot coals, but licked all over by translucent black flames.

'Thank you, my son, for all you've done to make restitution for my deeds. You've won me reprieve from the worst of my punishment. Alas, though, I'm yet chastised by these cold flames on account of all the tithes I never paid.'

'I'll see what I can do. But give me your pledge again that you'll appear to me in another fourteen days.'

The youth now had neither gold nor houses, neither land nor livestock – only his home in Redcliffe Street. He sold the house, but the sum it realised was not enough, so he returned to the honest merchant.

'Sir, I have nowhere else to turn. May I beg of you a loan of a hundred marks?'

The merchant was astounded that the lad could already have squandered the £2,000 he'd paid him. 'You have fallen in with scoundrels, I perceive, and lost your fortune on cards and dice!'

'It is not so, believe me.' Even now the youth couldn't bring himself to speak of his father's punishment. 'Only lend me the money and I shall be bondservant to you and your heirs as long as I live.'

Truly, the merchant loved him as if he were his own son. 'You ask me to loan you a hundred marks. I give you £100. I ask only this: that you use the money wisely, as there's no more I can give you.'

The youth took the £100 and the proceeds from his house and set out on a pilgrimage to one after another of the parishes, in Bristol and the shires beyond, where his father had held property or done business. At each church he paid the tithes his father had withheld. Soon enough all the money was gone, the tithes were paid, and the youth didn't know what else to do except trudge on foot back to the city.

On the road through the fields between Mangotsfield and Bristol, he was accosted by an old man in rags who recognised whose son he was and had heard about the restitution he'd been paying. 'Your father did mumble I out of the price on a dozen bushels of corn. Will 'ee pay me what he do rightly owe?'

'I'm sorry; all my money is spent. I can pay you only with this' – and the youth took off his fine doublet and gave it to the speechless old man.

He arrived in Bristol on the fourteenth day. He had no home to go to, so it was on Redcliffe Backs, where herring gulls wheeled about the boats moored to the quay, that he fell on his knees to pray.

This time it began with lovely music, like a symphony of the sounds of seashore and wood, meadow and moor, and a fragrance like a minster full of flowers, and then came a brilliant light, brighter than the brightest summer day, and a vision of a naked youth, beautiful and radiant.

'Are you my father?'

'I am. Because of what you've done for me, all my debts are paid, all my iniquity cleansed. I thank you from the bottom of my heart, my son. I give you my blessing, and I beg you release me from any pledge to return to this mortal world.'

Rejoicing to have received his father's blessing, the son set him free. With a flash of dazzling light the father's spirit shot to heaven.

But in Bristol the night was coming. The youth shivered in his shirt and watched the gulls squabbling over scraps of fish. He was cold, hungry and penniless. There was nowhere he could go – except back to the house of the honest merchant, who was dismayed to see him so grubby and gaunt, and shivering in his shirtsleeves.

'I have nothing,' said the youth. 'I cannot repay my debt. I come to yield myself as your bondservant.'

Yet still the merchant loved him. He could not make him his bondservant. 'Tell me, truly, how it has come about that you have lost all your wealth and been reduced to such penury.'

At last the youth was willing that the truth be told. He explained how he'd spent everything, even the doublet on his back, to make atonement for his father's deeds so his father's soul could be saved to enter heaven.

The merchant wept. 'I will not make you my bondservant. I will make you my partner in business.'

And so he did. The lawyer's son and the merchant together ran a company that everyone trusted as the last word in fair and honest trade. The merchant made the lad more than his partner. He made him his heir, since he had no son or daughter of his own. He introduced him to a friend's lovely daughter who became his wife. When he died he left the young man all his wealth. It may not have been so great a fortune as the lad had inherited from his father, but it was enough to set him up to live a happy and prosperous life.

Twenty-five

THE SEVENTH BRIDE

One warm May Day morning, young Polly was sewing in the rose bower when she heard the clip-clop and rattle of a carriage on the road outside the hedge. The noise abruptly stopped, and Polly thought nothing of that – till a shadow fell across her embroidery and there before her stood a man, smiling courteously. He looked well-to-do, in dark travelling clothes.

'Shall I show you to my father?'

'It's not for him I'm here.' The man's voice was deep and dry as stone. His eyes were crystalline grey. 'I glimpsed you through the hedge, my lady. I was smitten by your beauty.' He fell on one knee and swept low his hat. 'My body and soul are yours to command.'

Polly's heart leapt into her throat. Never had any young fellow spoken to her like this. Not that this gentleman was exactly young.

'Sir …' she stuttered, 'I do not even know you …'

'What is that if our hearts are predestined for each other?' The man stepped closer. His presence seemed to fill the bower. 'Do you not feel what I feel?'

She could not deny it. Her chest, her loins palpitated with feelings she'd never felt before. The man sat right down beside her and took her hand in his. 'How lovely the pink bloom of your cheeks, like the spirit of dawn enrobed in flesh!' Such words of enchantment he wove! When at last he kissed her lips, her heart was his.

'Will you come with me, my love, this very day, this very hour? Come with me to my castle in the North Country and I shall make you my bride!'

'Yes, my love … I will.'

'Make haste then, for the journey is far. Go to your room and put on your best clothes and jewels. Only your most precious things. Be quick, be stealthy, and meet me in my carriage on the road.'

Polly stepped softly so Father in his study would not hear. With thudding heart and shaking hands, she changed into her finest holland smock and silken stays and over that her best silk gown. At her throat and breast and on her fingers and in her hair she put on her most precious jewels.

But as she stole back down the hallway there came a croaking voice: 'Sweet Polly, won't you ask your father's leave before you sneak away so silent like a thief?'

It was Father's parrot, on his perch in the corner.

'Hush!' Polly whispered. 'I will not ask my father's leave, for my heart has spoken and I must do what I desire.'

In the waiting carriage, beside her betrothed, she took her seat. He cracked the whip, and the horses – one white, one grey – sprang forwards to carry them away.

With a wild laugh she cried, 'I don't even know your name!'

'My name is Sir John,' he said.

North and east he drove her along the dusty Cotswold roads. They travelled late into that long May evening, till an hour before sunset they came to a gateway, and along a winding track through trees, to a splendid flat-topped building. A pillared loggia framed its entrance, and a long green sward swept away like a racetrack.

'Is this your castle then, Sir John?'

'It's a long journey yet to the North Country, but here we may spend our wedding night, my sweet' – and Polly flushed to think of the pleasures soon to come.

No servant came to greet them, only a leggy black hound that raced barking from the trees. Fearsome though he looked, the dog gambolled and slavered in joy when Sir John fussed and patted him. The man unlocked the door. The dog bounded ahead into the echoey stone-paved hall with stags' heads mounted on every wall. Sir John locked the door behind them and put the key back in his pocket.

'Is there no one here?' asked Polly.

'Only you and me, my love. At this late hour the servants have gone, but I know my way around.'

He lit a candle and led the way down to the basement kitchen. The hound sniffed around while Sir John searched out platters of bread and cheese and fruit.

'I must choose a vintage from the wine cellar to celebrate our wedding. Why don't you look around upstairs?'

Once she was alone, the force of Sir John's spell on Polly's heart began to soften. If she were to leave this strange empty building right now, and borrow a horse, she'd be home before morning and Father could be convinced she'd come back late from an outing, and everything would be as it was before. The main door she knew was locked. By the fading light through the windows she found her way to a back door. But that was locked too.

Turning round, she almost tripped over the hound. He glanced up as if beckoning her. So she followed him, back down the steps, past the glow of light from the wine cellar and into the kitchen gloom, to the door of what she guessed to be a larder. The dog's interest in it made her curious. She lit a candle from the embers in the fireplace, opened the door – and started back at the high smell and bristly headless carcass of a deer hanging from a hook. But as she was closing the door she spotted the low shadowy entrance of what looked like a passage. Some route perhaps by which to bring in the venison? It was now or never. Sir John would come any moment with the wine. She stepped inside, closed the door on the dog, and ducked past the headless carcass into the passageway.

Bent double like a crippled crone, holding out the candle to light the way, Polly stumbled along the passage. It continued far beyond the few yards needed to be past the building's walls. It was faced with brick at first, but soon became bare earth and rock. She could hear the trickle of water all around. Her shoes sank into mud. When she stopped to rest, the air was deathly cold.

Having come so far, she struggled on, till something pale showed ahead. What it was she couldn't tell. Only when she was very near did she realise that the passage opened into a wider cavity and that the pale object extended beyond the tunnel's width. Her first thought was that it was another deer carcass, shaven bare. Then she thought it was a slender pig. But the candlelight couldn't deny the truth. It was the naked body of a young woman, pristine white, unblemished by any wound. Lovely were her ashen features, and long and black was her hair. Beyond her, topped and toed by crude stone slabs, lay another woman's body, whose skin was just as pale, whose nails and hair were longer. Deeper in the gloom beyond lay another … and another … Six naked white bodies lay in that underground

chamber, each one further back with nails and hair longer grown than the one before. In the shadows behind the last was a dead end of stone and earth.

Polly trembled in terror in the icy air. There was nothing else she could do but tortuously retrace her steps. As she emerged into the kitchen she heard Sir John calling her name from somewhere upstairs. She wanted with all her heart to believe he had no knowledge of those dead maidens, but she dared not let him know where she'd been. She took off her muddy shoes and hid them in the firewood. Up three flights of stairs she clambered – and found him in a large, high-ceilinged room. Shadows crossed the floor from a pair of candles and the last of the day's light through the windows opposite the fireplace, where the hound demurely sat.

'There you are!' Polly cried.

Sir John stared her up and down. His gaze seemed to linger on her feet. 'Where have you been all this time?'

'Oh, looking around.' She gestured wildly at the tapestries on the wall. 'What a marvellous house this is!'

He handed her a glass of wine and took her out on the loggia roof. The air outside was still warm. Shreds of fiery red streaked the sky above the mile-long course where dogs would test their speed against the deer. Polly looked down to the ground below. Too big a drop to jump.

'Do the dogs here kill the deer?' she asked.

'They do when it's a fleshing course.'

He placed his arm around her waist and led her back inside. She sipped the wine. She nibbled some cheese, though it caught in her throat.

At last he took her hands and gazed piercingly into her eyes. 'Are you ready now to be wed, my love?'

Still the man's enchantment worked its magic. The wine had swum to her head. Her heartbeat skipped and jumped. She tried not to think of those six white bodies buried beneath the earth.

She said, 'Are there … bedchambers … in this lodge?'

'It's a warm May Day night, when lovers should sport beneath the stars.'

He led her down to the rear hall and unlocked the back door. 'Won't you wear your shoes, my dear?'

Her heart skipped a beat. 'I want to feel the earth on my naked feet.'

He gripped her hand tight as they passed through the wood behind the lodge. The hound flitted like a shadow from tree to tree. Polly stifled her gasps when sharp sticks pricked her bare soles. The sky was filled with stars when at last they emerged into an open field, dotted with twisting oaks … and a large grassy mound.

'What's that, Sir John?'

'Just an ancient barrow.' His hand gripped hers tighter. When she looked again to the barrow the black dog was perched atop it, silhouetted against the night.

The field descended to a stream that was in full spate after April's rains. Sir John led Polly between the hawthorns and reeds to its marshy edge, cold and wet on her feet. He turned her to face him and let go her hand.

'This is the place, sweet Polly.'

She held up her face to be kissed —

'Take off your fine jewels, my dear. Take off your silken gown.'

There was the rushing stream behind her, the reeds and thorns each side, and in front of her stood Sir John and the steep slope beyond. From fingers and hair, from throat and breast, she plucked off her jewels and laid them in the grass. She loosened her gown and let its fine silk crumple to her feet.

'Now take off your silken stays, my love.'

She unlaced her corset and pulled it free and flung it down.

'Take off your holland smock, my sweet.'

With trembling hands she took the smock by its hem and pulled it over her head. Naked and white she shivered in the night's warm breeze and Sir John's crystal gaze, and knew she was as lovely as any of those six maidens lying cold inside the barrow.

'Will you give me now your love?' she said.

'Step into the stream, my dear, and wash your soiled feet.'

What could she do? Where could she go? But backward one step, still facing him and gasping as chill water came to her knees.

'Tell me truly, Sir John, was it only for my jewels and fine clothes that you wanted me as your bride?'

'Step a little deeper, my love, so your loins may be cleansed.'

She took another step backwards – and cried out as the rushing, tugging water came right up to her hips.

'Take my jewels and clothes, Sir John! Take everything you want! Only let me out now, please, because this water is cold and deep.'

'Step a little deeper, my sweet, and then you'll be my bride.'

On the water's edge he towered high above her like a black-cloaked god. One corner of her heart yet clung to the hope he might mean that promise. She took one more step backwards, the stream engulfed her to the shoulders, and she hardly had the strength to brace herself against its force.

'O Sir John, tell me truly: those six maids who lie cold in the barrow, was each one of them your bride?'

'True enough,' he said, 'and you will be the seventh.'

'Then will you not give me one kiss to comfort me on my wedding night?' She begged him with all the power of her starlit eyes. She rallied her strength for one step back towards the bank, and the water streamed down from her young white breasts.

Into the spate stepped Sir John, in his boots and trousers, tunic and cloak. Water soaked into the heavy fabric as he seized the girl's shoulders and pressed his lips to her mouth. She kissed him fiercely back and wrapped her wet white arms round him. For a moment she felt him relax. With all her strength she hurled him into the current. The weight of his boots and waterlogged clothes dragged him down, while Polly swam naked for the bank. Two strong strokes and she was out, dripping and shivering, as Sir John flailed and yelled.

'Help me, Polly! Help me and I promise I'll marry you!'

'You've drowned six young brides, Sir John. Now be husband to them all!'

He sank gurgling under and she pulled on her smock. His hands stabbed out, snatching at the air, as she tied on her stays. His head burst gasping above water and she put on her silk gown.

Then he sank out of sight and she picked up her jewels and hurried back, past the barrow and waiting hound, and through the woods, to the lodge.

On the white horse from Sir John's carriage she rode through the night, till an hour before sunrise she made it home. The house was silent and dark, save one lantern left burning in the hall. Steal silently to bed, she thought, and Father will never be the wiser where you've been or what you've done.

But as she crossed the hall a voice in the corner croaked, 'You must have been with a bad rogue, Polly, to tarry out so late.'

That parrot, loud enough to wake the dead!

From upstairs came Father's sleepy voice: 'Why is that parrot prattling at such an ungodly hour?'

Polly glared at the parrot.

The parrot looked boldly back and called out nice and loud, 'A cat came and cornered me; I was afraid that he'd have me … but now he is gone.'

'For those words,' whispered Polly, 'I'll have you made a beautiful golden cage with an ivory door, to keep you safe from any harm.'

'O Polly,' said the parrot, 'does it have to be a cage?'

Twenty-six

THE WISH BOTTLE

One fine evening Dick Carroll was fishing from the quayside in Gloucester Docks. He was with his mate Bert, a retired sailor, and the fishing wasn't going well. When at last Dick caught something, it was just an old bottle, empty and unlabelled.

'Bugger!' said Dick – 'I wish I'd caught a fish' – and threw the bottle back in the water.

Two unexpected things then happened. A fish suddenly appeared on the end of his line – and the bottle reappeared on the quay beside his foot.

'Ha!' said Bert. 'That's a wish bottle, that is.' He indicated the faint swirling shadow inside. 'There's the demon as makes it work.'

'What do you mean, a "wish bottle"?'

'A wish bottle gives each person as owns it one wish, whatever they want. But if you still have the bottle when you die then the demon will snatch your soul to hell. Only way you can get shot of it is by selling it for less than you bought it.'

'How do you know this?' asked Dick, who was starting to feel jittery.

'I were a sailor, weren't I? If you travel the world you learn all kinds of things.'

'Well, I never bought it.' Dick flung the bottle as hard as he could into the harbour basin.

They never even heard a splash. There was the bottle back by his foot.

Bert said, 'I reckon as because you did make a wish you are its owner now. And because you got it without buying it you can set the price as whatever you like. Only it'll need to be low enough to get a buyer in the first place and high enough not to seem too tricky to sell on.'

What Dick needed was a pint. So they adjourned to the British Flag – or the Tall Ship, as it's known today. They say it was the kind of pub where you had your first drink and you had your last drink. As Dick sipped his first drink he realised how he'd wasted his chance at a wish. One little fish, when he could have had anything.

'Tell you what, Bert, why don't you buy the bottle off me, have a wish, and then sell the bottle back to me so I can have a proper go before I get shot of it?'

Bert was silent a minute, then he said, 'All right. How much do you want for it?'

'How much have you got?'

Bert fingered through his wallet. 'Ninety quid – plus coppers.'

'Is that all?' Dick was thinking that a bit more would give a better margin of safety.

'It's all I have on me.'

Bert handed over the money and Dick handed over the bottle.

'I wish', said Bert, 'that I had a really swish, brand new ocean-going yacht.'

They waited. Nothing seemed to have happened.

'Well, it's not going to appear inside the bloody pub!' said Bert. They craned their heads to look through the window and there in the Victoria Basin, gleaming in the low-angled sun, was a very nice yacht.

'Is that all you wanted?'

'It's what I've dreamed of, so I can travel the world again – as a free agent.'

Dick bought the bottle back. For £89.

'I wish … that I had £1 million.'

Straightaway a huge stack of £50 notes appeared on the table. Everyone in the pub stared in amazement. Dick had to buy a double round of drinks, and then he explained about the wish bottle. There was quite a bit of interest, but hesitation too. In the end it was the landlord who bought it, for £88. He held back from making a wish right then – 'I'm going to think carefully about this' – and put the bottle on a shelf above the bar.

Dick had a missus and a baby daughter, Helen. When it came to spending the money, he was amazed how quickly it went, and wished he'd asked for more. They bought a nice house with a bit of land in the Forest of Dean. On a sunny day the place was like a kind of paradise. For several years they had a very nice life.

Until, when Helen was nine years old, she fell sick. It was meningitis. The doctors did everything they could, but it wasn't enough and Dick knew his little girl was going to die. £1 million was nothing compared with Helen's life. He wished he'd kept the wish bottle for a time like this when he really needed it. Maybe that was the kind of reason the landlord of the British Flag hadn't made a wish straight away. Dick drove down to Gloucester docks, rushed into the pub, but the bottle was gone.

'I sold it to a bloke from New York, for £87' – and the landlord gave Dick the man's address.

'Did you make a wish?' asked Dick before he left.

'Oh yes,' said the landlord, with a twinkle in his eye, but he wouldn't say what.

Across the Atlantic went Dick, to a penthouse at the top of a skyscraper on Broadway. The man had wished for $1 billion, set himself up in an international business, and was making billions more every year – which made Dick wonder why he hadn't just wished for more money in the first place. He didn't have the wish bottle any more. He'd sold it to someone from Pittsburgh.

So Dick followed the bottle's trail across America, the price of purchase steadily decreasing each time it had moved on. The man in Pittsburgh had wished for the love of a woman he'd adored for twenty-five years, but mostly people had wished for huge amounts of dosh. Dick felt a bit sheepish that his own wish – the second one – had been so predictable and that he'd asked for so modest a sum. The amounts these Americans had wished for had increased the money supply so much that the whole country was suffering inflation. There were exceptions, though. A woman in Dallas had wished she'd never lose her looks. A boy in Thermopolis, Wyoming, had wished for an endless supply of chocolate. A pastor in Tucson had wished to know for sure whether God really exists. A hippie in Marin County, California, had wished that the land around her little commune would never get ruined by development.

From California the trail crossed the ocean to Hawaii; the price of the bottle ever smaller and smaller. An old Kanaka on the Big Island had wished for reconciliation between his two sons who'd fallen out. A scientist in Honolulu had wished that no more of the native birds of Oahu would become extinct. Island-hopping westwards Dick travelled, till the trail led to Kauai, and the west coast of that garden island, the extremity of the inhabited zone, and a café-bar overlooking the sea. Flowers filled the garden with colour and the air with scent. Birds sang in the candlenut trees, waves rushed on the shore, and the setting sun was reflected as a wobbly golden line across the sea. A gorgeous Hawaiian woman with a hibiscus in her hair welcomed Dick with an ice-cold beer.

'All my life I wanted to have a bar in a beautiful place overlooking the sea,' said the haole from Kansas who owned this bar. He had an air of deep melancholy and a haunted look in his eyes. In a corner behind the counter stood the bottle. Dick could see the swirling shadow of the demon inside.

'How much did you pay for it?'

'Two cents.'

'*Two cents?*'

'Yeah, I know. No one will ever buy it, I'm doomed to hell, but at the time, when the dream was in reach, that seemed not to matter so much as to live the dream while I could …'

Dick thought of his daughter lying sick at home. His daughter who meant more to him than anything. He eyed the shifting shadow inside the bottle. What else could he do? To the barkeeper's astonishment he bought the bottle for one cent. He made his wish at once, and when he got home to the Forest little Helen came running to the gate to hug him. He was so glad to see her well, he'd surely made the right decision, but when he went to bed that night he regarded once again the shadow churning inside the bottle by his bed. As he watched, the shadow darkened and then spilled out of the bottle, bigger and bigger, to become a hideous winged being with eyes and breath of fire.

'Now you are mine!' the demon roared, and all through the night it tormented him with the horror of what awaited him in hell. Till at last he woke up and it was morning, and there beside the bed was the wish bottle with a faint swirling shadow inside and all he could think of was the terror of waiting through all the days and nights that lay ahead.

What he needed was a pint. So down to Gloucester he went, to see his old mates at the British Flag. Bert was there, tanned and wizened from yachting round the world. Alone in the corner sat a hard case no one had ever dared to speak to, arms blackened with tattoos, and drinking whisky like beer.

Bert said to Dick, 'Why you looking so down in the mouth?'

Dick told the whole story and how he'd bought the wish bottle for one American cent to save his daughter's life. He placed the bottle on the table. Everyone stared at it with dread. They said what a shame it was, and all of them silently thanked the stars it wasn't their own soul the bottle demon had won.

You'll remember I said the British Flag was the kind of pub where you had your first drink and you had your last drink.

It was customary to pay for your last drink with whatever change you had left; you'd drop it in the big jar on the counter. So this jar was full of coins of many different nations, left by seamen from all over the world. In the silence after Dick had told his story, the hard case in the corner suddenly lurched to his feet, swayed across the room, lifted the jar of change, and smashed it on the floor. Coins scattered everywhere. The man stooped down and picked out the tiniest, most worthless one there was: a Turkish lira.

'I reckons as that's worth less than an American cent.' He handed the coin to Dick. 'There you are, mate. I'm going to hell anyway, so I'll take that bottle off your hands.'

Since the man spent most of his time in the pub, the bottle was kept for him on the shelf above the bar. He'll be dead by now, and in hell, unless God has power to change the rules. On that shelf, so the story goes, the wish bottle has stood ever since.

When I went in the Tall Ship, as the pub's now called, and asked about the bottle, the landlady didn't know what I meant. So I told her the gist of the story.

'I've never heard about that before,' she said, 'but there are plenty of bottles up there.'

I took a step backwards, looked up, and on a shelf high above the bar was a row of fifty old bottles, all of them empty and unlabelled.

Twenty-seven

THE FAIRY HORN

Will Robbins was out gathering mushrooms in the Forest. He'd caught himself a rabbit too. The verderers would have something to say if they knew about that. The way Will saw it, he was a Forester born and bred and he had as much right to bag a rabbit as anyone else born in the hundred of St Briavels. It wasn't like he was hunting the King's deer.

It was the tag end of summer, a warm sticky day, and Will couldn't guess how far he'd walked, back and forth, round and about, in search of mushrooms. He was hot, tired and thirsty, and right in the centre of the Forest, so he'd a long walk home yet to do. Now Will knew the Forest as well as any mortal man. He knew there was a place very near where you could quench your thirst. He'd been there before. Not often, mind. You wouldn't want to go there too often.

So he turned his steps through the oak woods of the Forest's deep heart. The sunshine lanced golden through the greenery, in which the first yellowing of fall could be discerned by a careful eye. Soon he was out of the trees and climbing a steep slope of bracken and furze. It was an almost conical hill, steep on all sides, rising higher than the oaks. At the summit a brake of birches shivered in the wind. Badger holes opened from among their roots. Up here you could see almost the whole Forest: a blanket of green treetops ruckled over ridge and valley, from Staple-edge to Purples Hill, broken here and there by patchwork strips of yellowy green pasture.

Will turned his face to the earth beneath the birches.

'I do thirst.'

Those were the words; the simple truth.

As if from nowhere, a young man appeared in front of him, a man dressed in the simple garb of a far-gone time: nettle cloth round his loins, and silver ornaments on his tawny throat and arms. In his hands was the horn: a long curving horn that had once, ages past, graced the head of a wild ox and now was jewelled with gold and gems.

Without a word the young man handed Will the horn. Just as each time Will had come here, it was heavy and full. He put it to his lips and drank. The taste was like the finest mead mixed with clear spring water and a splash of the old gods' nectar. Its coolness tingled through his veins and at once his mind was alert, his limbs supple, as if he'd shed the weight of ten years.

Will handed back the horn, nodded his thanks, and a moment later the young man vanished as if the hill had swallowed him. With a smile on his face, Will ambled down through the bracken and furze, all zesty now to get back to Nelly and see how much she loved him for bringing home a rabbit.

Something white flashed through the oak trunks below. Will glimpsed it again: a stag with a fine pair of antlers, flitting away like a ghost, so creamy pale his hide. A minute later, as Will reached the bottom of the hill, there crashed into view a nobleman riding on a bay mare and cloaked in blue. Both horse and knight looked exhausted. The poor mare's flanks glistened with sweat.

The man called to Will in a well-born accent of the North: 'Did you see a white stag come by?'

'I did, sir, but too far ahead on you to catch him.' That much was plain from the state of the mare. 'May I say, sir, you be bold to be a-hunting the King's deer.'

The knight slid like a sack of turnips from the saddle. 'And you, my man, are bold to say so. The King has granted me one head by way of payment for a service.'

Will thought of that stag's fine head mounted in the hall of a manor – and how many days the meat on a stag's carcass would last to feed his family and neighbours.

The knight wiped his sweaty brow. 'Do you carry any water?'

Will shook his head and hoped the bag in which he'd stowed the rabbit didn't draw the nobleman's eye.

'I've heard there's a place around here', said the knight, 'where a man can get a most invigorating refreshment.'

It was no secret to keep from one in need. 'Yes, sir. Such do be anighst.' And Will told him where to go and what to say.

The knight tethered his horse and up the hill he went, almost swooning with fatigue. He paid no regard to the view, but straight away said the words: 'I do thirst.'

At once the young man appeared with that treasure of a horn. The knight of the north drank and drank till the horn was dry. In a trice his strength returned. He felt better and brighter than he'd done for years. He held up the horn before his eyes. How precious and fine its decoration! How marvellous the effect of drinking from it!

The tawny young man in nettle cloth and silver jewels must have seen the look in the knight's eyes. He held out open hands to receive the horn back. But the knight would not return it.

'Thou must give back the horn!' cried the young man in an accent arcane and strange.

The knight clutched the horn tight and fled down the hill, tripping and leaping through the bracken and furze. As he ran, an unearthly scream, like a woman's shriek of rage, ripped through the air and shuddered through the ground beneath his speeding feet. In reply there came a blizzard of other yells, sharp grating cries like the utterance of trees in a gale. The knight leapt astride his horse and spurred her away as fast as that tired nag could go.

He could hear the quick crunching of their steps. From the corners of his eyes he glimpsed the figures bursting from the trees. The whole wood seemed alive as a wind picked up and rushed and rattled through the branches.

Will Robbins watched the knight go, saw the horn he clutched. He hid low in the ferns and held his breath as the chase went by, whip-thin figures as brown as bark, screaming with the fury of a storm. Down through the oaks they pursued the knight into the valley of a brook, the horse careering too fast, exhausted, out of control, the rider's blue cloak billowing out behind. Suddenly, near the stream, the mare stumbled, the rider was flung through the air – and smacked head first into the ground. The mare recovered her stride and raced on. The knight lay still. The wind dropped as abruptly as it had come. The spiky dark figures melted into the trees as if they'd never been. Dead silence hung in the air.

Will made his way warily down to the spot. He could feel the prickle of wild fairy eyes watching from every bush. The blue-draped body of the knight remained quite still. A trickle of scarlet ran from his temple. One arm lay outflung towards the stream, the other bent beneath the cloak. The horn was not in sight.

With the jingling and squeaking of bridle tack, a column of horsemen came riding down the path beside the stream: a dozen men-at-arms and at their head a stern red-haired lord dressed in green. The Earl of Gloucester, no less, en route to St Briavel's Castle.

No sooner did the men-at-arms behold the situation than they spurred forwards to surround Will, swords bristling from their hands. There he was, a humble churl alone with a dead knight at his feet and a rabbit in his bag.

The Earl jumped down and looked at the wound on the dead man's head and then he looked at Will. 'So, what have you got to say?'

'He did take the fairy horn.'

Now the Earl had the skill to read a man's face and know if he were honest or false. He knew enough, too, of the lore of his lands to understand the meaning of Will's words. He rolled over the dead knight's body ... and there, gripped beneath his arm, was the glittering gold-trimmed horn. The Earl lifted it in his hands and he too felt the desire to keep this treasure as his own.

Will saw the look in the Earl's eyes. He thought of those lithe brown figures behind each bush and tree, their fierce gaze trained upon this little group of horsemen, upon the horn in the Earl of Gloucester's hands, as they waited to see what he would do.

The Earl said to Will, 'Do you know the place where it came from?'

Will nodded.

The Earl hesitated a heartbeat longer, then placed the horn in Will's hands. 'Take it back where it belongs.'

By the time Will Robbins got back up the hill, the sun was setting into the serried treetops in the west and the evening star was shining. The birches at the summit were tall dark figures hunched against the chill of dusk. Will stood in the spot where he'd said the words before. But this time he already held the fairy horn.

He tried the only thing he knew: 'I do thirst.'

Nothing happened; the words were a lie. What was he to do?

The sun was sinking out of sight. Soon it would be night, and the fairy folk were abroad. He could feel their gaze upon his back. The empty horn seemed a great weight in his hands. The last red sliver of sun slipped down, shooting sparks between the tips of the trees. In that same moment the ground shuddered beneath his feet, and one of the badger holes began to unfunnel, bigger and bigger till he could see right in, past crumbling earth and snaky roots, to a cave inside the hill. The fiery sunset light gleamed from a pair of eyes in the gloom … and a black jungle of hair, piercing sharp features, and a torc of gold round a tawny throat … a woman, who with a lordly gesture beckoned Will within.

An earthy odour filled his lungs as he stepped inside the cave. At any moment, he feared, the walls of the hill might seal behind him. The lady beckoned him closer. He could smell her scent of nettle and thyme. Her thin lips twisted into a grim ghost of a smile. She held out one long bony hand, Will gave up the horn, and her other hand whipped up to catch his wrist.

'Wilt thou stay awhile, Will, and drink and dine with us?'

Whip-thin men and women appeared all round him as if straight from the dank stone walls. A young man took the horn from the lady and withdrew into the shadows beyond, where a noise of trickling liquid echoed. A woman proffered a dish of nuts and berries. Will had a breathless feeling the walls were already closing round him. It was one thing to drink from the fairy horn; another to partake of any food inside the hollow hill.

He thought of the rabbit in his bag, and Nelly. 'Thank you, mam, but I best be a-wending.'

He turned away through the gauntlet of wild-eyed folk and out from the earth into the lambent twilight. When he looked back, the hill had closed, only badger holes now beneath the birches, and everything was as before. Will muttered a quick prayer and sped away home through the night.

He never went back and said the words to beg another draught from the horn. There were others who tried, of course, and the hill is still there, planted over with pines, but never again since that day has a tawny young man come forth with the fairy horn to grant any mortal a taste of the world beyond.

Twenty-eight

THE UNCHRISTENED BABE

It was past noon when the young mother came to the little church on the hill. Her face was streaked with tears, her hair unbound, and to her bosom she clutched a lifeless bundle. The priest was alone at his prayers. He scowled at the disturbance when the door creaked open, and scowled all the more when he saw who it was.

'My baby … will you bury my baby?'

The priest glared at the woman's pale features, her uncovered hair, and the unshriven creature in her arms.

'I wonder that you dare step inside this temple of the Lord – you in whose house the heretic's cursed book was found, you whose husband God has judged for leading other men astray. I will not bury your offspring on consecrated ground. That is the law for those who die unbaptised, outside the arms of God's holy Church.'

Weeping all the more, the mother turned away. Mr Tyndale's New Testament had been her Joseph's most treasured possession; as a boy, he'd once met the great scholar when he lived at Little Sodbury Manor. The book's sacred words had given her the courage to keep going when Joseph's boat failed to return from sea and she had to struggle on alone with a baby on the way. Surely a good man like Joseph had not deserved God's wrath. And surely the baby, who'd lived but a few hours, was innocent of any offence.

In her humble cottage she laid the infant's body in the crib. She felt so alone. She didn't know what to do. So she fell on her knees and prayed for her unchristened babe, that he would not be condemned to a godless eternal hell. She prayed for some crumb of comfort in the midst of her desolation. Exhausted by lack of sleep all the terrible night past, she dropped at last into the mercy of sleep, and dreamt.

There were trees and flowers of brilliant sunlit colours, and white clouds sailing the blue heavens, and a view down to a river's deeper blue, and everywhere the music of birdsong and wind. On a mossy ledge sat Joseph, more radiant and youthful than she ever remembered him, all the cares of his life softened from his brow. On his knee the squirming baby squealed with joy and waved his little hands and feet in the air. Then the two of them together looked up at her with love.

As the priest meanwhile returned to his house, he felt compelled, to justify what he'd done. The rules of the Church must be obeyed. The woman was a heretic like her husband. There was no place for their kind in God's kingdom. The daylight dimmed and the priest knelt by his bed to pray. His conscience was distracted, he kept losing track of his words, till at last he heard a voice from within cut across his grasshoppering mind, saying strong and clear, 'Go from your room and behold the unburied dead!'

With trembling hands the priest opened the door. On the hall floor sprawled the body of his servant, breathless and still. In the kitchen the maid was slumped against the wall, sightless eyes staring. The priest yelped in terror and rushed outside and through the dark trees to Hill Court. The house was silent and pervaded by a sickly sweet smell. He stumbled from room to room: the servants, master, lady, children all lay dead where they'd fallen. Even the dog lay stiff beside the hearth.

The priest fled to the church, to the sanctuary of holy ground. But as he passed through the gate a pungent stench tugged at his guts. In the crepuscular light he saw piled between the yews dozens of corpses, expelled from their graves, in different states of decay according to the lapse of time since their death. Sightless sockets stared at him. In the mouldering flesh, peeling from the bone, maggots and worms burrowed and curled.

Down the hill the priest ran; but the grass in the fields was seared, the summer flowers had shrivelled, and here and there lay the bloated carcasses of sheep, legs jutting up at the darkened sky, and little corpses of birds at the feet of gaunt leafless trees. From the hamlet of Hill came a strong stink of death, so he steered well clear of the houses and sped on down the wasted fields till he reached the Severn's bank. But the very waters of the river had dried up, to leave a shiny scar of mud where the stranded bodies of salmon and shad lay rotting. He staggered along the bank, desperate to escape his death-cursed parish, but the darkness stiffened around him, became a pall of black in which he couldn't see which way to flee, could only grope on hands and knees, whining, weeping, till his fingers closed on something cool, soft, still – a baby's corpse lying unburied in the darkness. Then the priest discovered that he too couldn't breathe. He too was dead, alone, abandoned in this godless night.

With a groan he woke in a sweat on his bedroom floor. For the rest of that night he brooded on the meaning of his dream. His mind festered with his guilt. When dawn came, he didn't know what to do except go to the church, where the graves lay blessedly intact. Then he saw a stooping figure in black trudge past the gate, heading uphill: the young mother with that pitiful bundle in her arms.

She didn't see the priest as he stepped from the churchyard to follow her. She didn't see the buttercups, orchids, clover she was trampling, or the butterflies skipping before her in erratic little squadrons. Clutching tight her burden, she scrambled down the gullies in Roundhouse Wood. In a spot of dappled shade among the hart's-tongue ferns, she dug with her bare hands a hole in the earth. She lined it with moss and flowers, like the gardens that little girls make for the fairies, and then placed her baby in. When she saw him lying in that leafy, petalled bed, her heart broke yet again. She lifted him out and held him close. So hard it was to let him go. At last she kissed him one last time and put him back in his grave, laid a coverlet of ferns over him, and shovelled in the earth.

She didn't know the words the priest would say. She spoke the words her heart gave her and hoped they'd be enough. 'O Lord, will you bless him wherever he's gone; keep him safe with his papa till I can come to him?' A sunbeam shone down through the branches on the grave, the wood pigeons cooed, and a blackbird fluted its melody of joy. 'Be a blessing to this wood, my little sweetheart. Your mama won't forget you. I'll come and bring you flowers and sit with you. Rest in peace, my little one, and may God give me peace too.'

Unseen by the mother, the priest watched and heard. As he listened to her prayer his conscience smote him like a sword. His hardened heart broke open. He stepped out from the thicket and fell on his knees at the woman's feet and wept. 'Forgive me, for I have sinned! I'm not worthy to be a priest. May God bless you and your child. May God hear your prayers.' And again he pleaded for forgiveness, and whether from God or from the mother it would be difficult to say.

As the tears ran down his face, he felt soft hands upon his crown. He closed his tear-stung eyes. The birdsong and the wind rang and whispered in his ears. The warm radiance of those hands spread down through his hair and skull, and flooded through his soul, and filled all the world.

'Peace be with you, Father,' came the woman's whisper.

The priest opened his eyes. 'And peace be with you.'

Twenty-nine

PUESDOWN INN

A cold wind was howling across the wolds when Greg and Sandy McConnor pulled up outside the Puesdown Inn. They were Australians and starting to wonder what had possessed them to visit England in November. In the inn's dark, moody parlour they could feel the weight of many centuries, despite the Pink Floyd playing on the radio cassette.

'Will that be a double room, sir?' said the landlord.

'No, a twin if you have one,' said Greg.

As usual, Sandy felt embarrassed about what the man might think. At least Greg had refrained from explaining that they needed separate beds to get a good night's sleep. Not that Sandy herself needed a separate bed to sleep.

'If you want anything in the night' – the landlord indicated the booze – 'help yourself and we'll add it on your tab in the morning.'

'Trusting guy,' said Greg as they climbed the stairs.

Sheets and blankets on the bed. No duvet. No en suite. You had to go along the corridor to the bathroom. While Greg showered, Sandy put on her nightie. It was a pretty one, but it didn't make her feel pretty.

Greg was already in his pyjamas when he came back.

'Hug?' she said.

He hugged her in his stiff, bearish way. She slipped her hands under the pyjamas and one thing led to another and soon they were on one of the beds.

'Take off your pyjamas?'

'Too cold.'

Maybe it wasn't hot by Australian standards, but the radiator was on and Sandy thought it cosy enough. Greg had the bit between his teeth. With an unbuttoning down there and a shoving up of the nightie here, it was soon over. When Greg had caught his breath, he moved to the other bed to read some more of his paperback, *Way Ahead on Productivity*, before he sank asleep. Sandy knew he wouldn't want to do it again for a week, when the tension would have built up in him again. She tried to remember how it had been when they were first married. Greg had been willing to give it more time, had been able to sleep soundly in bed with her, before his job got so all-consuming and he started moving up the ladder. How much longer, she wondered, could they carry on like this?

In the middle of the night, Greg was woken by three loud dramatic knocks on the door downstairs. They had tremendous urgency, like someone was desperate to get in. Who on earth could that be at such a crazy hour? Then silence again but for the steady rhythm of Sandy's breathing. Greg was wide awake. The room had got quite warm. He started thinking about work, how behind he was going to be.

It was hopeless. He picked up his book and sweater and went downstairs, switching on lights as he went. From the windows near the front door he peered out into the night. No one there. He helped himself to a double shot of Scotch and settled in an armchair by the smouldering remains of the fire to sip the whisky and read. The book talked about how to keep a subliminal sense of fear among the workforce – the feeling you might get fired at any time – so as to optimise productivity. There were great data from Japan to prove that it really did work.

Suddenly he felt a weird icy presence brush behind his head.
He jerked round. Nothing there; only the bar, where the firelight
glittered on the metalwork and glass. But he could still detect a
presence. Nothing he could see. It was more as if he could *feel* it
as it moved away past the bar and up the stairs.

'To hell with that!' He turned back to his book.

A little later he heard a creaking overhead – old floorboards
creaking with the steps of someone moving along the corridor.
Maybe Sandy going to the loo? Was anyone else staying here
tonight? Where were the landlord's rooms? Greg discovered he'd
read the same paragraph three times. He realised the footsteps
couldn't have been Sandy's because they weren't going in the
right direction for the bathroom. And he hadn't heard them
coming back the other way.

Sandy, meanwhile, was dreaming. Someone needed help, there
was somebody she was trying desperately to save, but they were
slipping away … and the dream was fading, and though she wasn't
fully awake yet either, she became aware of the bedclothes being
peeled back and felt a draught of air on her arm. Then something
cold slid in alongside her.

'Greg?'

She wasn't sure whether she was pleased he wanted to be in
bed with her or annoyed that he should be so icy cold. Maybe

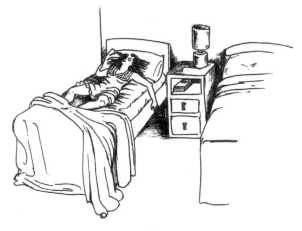

she should try to warm him up. She twisted about, blindly extended one arm, and drifted back asleep.

When Greg returned to the room he found it stiflingly warm. He tiptoed through the darkness and fumbled with the radiator. Once his eyes had adjusted, he saw the bedclothes pulled away from Sandy's sleeping form, her nightdress rucked up so one hip was bare. He hovered beside the bed, unsure whether to pull the bedclothes back over her.

'Greg?' Her face turned sleepily towards him. 'You didn't have to get out. You can stay in with me.'

Plainly she'd been dreaming. 'Sandy, have you been up and about? To the dunny or anything?'

'No. Just sleeping.'

At breakfast Greg told the landlord what drink he'd had in the night. 'Just the one … It felt kind of weird down here.'

'"Weird", sir?' A ghost of a smile played on the landlord's face.

Greg observed that none of the other tables was laid for breakfast. 'Thought I heard someone tramping about upstairs.'

'Not me.' Again that inscrutable smile.

The couple spent the day sightseeing in nearby Cotswold villages. Greg didn't give them much attention. He seemed to Sandy more than usually absent from the world around him, and he was tired from lack of sleep. In Bourton-on-the-Water he bought the *Financial Times* to help keep himself up to speed. What he really wanted was to be somewhere he could phone his office in Brisbane without needing a ton of 10p pieces.

'Why don't we head on to Cheltenham tonight instead of staying another night in that creepy inn?'

'I like the inn,' said Sandy. 'It's got character. And the room was really cosy.'

After dinner that night, Sandy nipped down the corridor to the bathroom in just a towel. She felt a bit self-conscious. There had been some young truck drivers taking dinner and she wasn't sure whether they were staying the night.

She got the shower running nice and hot. Had to work vigorously with the soap because the water was so hard. As she showered she began to get a strange feeling that someone was the other side of the curtain. Had she bolted the door? She couldn't remember. She wasn't used to these shared bathrooms.

'Greg?'

No reply.

She carried on soaping herself and letting the shower rinse down the suds. She still had that feeling someone was there. The curtain was too opaque to see through. She toyed with the idea of suddenly whipping it back. The thought gave her a thrum of excitement.

When she'd finished, she slowly peered round the curtain. No one there. But when she stepped out of the shower an icy chill tingled on her skin.

In the bedroom she found Greg reading that book.

'Did you come in the bathroom just now, honey?'

Greg noticed the flush of pink in his wife's tan. 'No. Why?'

'Just wondered.'

When he went to brush his teeth, the bathroom was still steamy from Sandy's shower and he had to wipe the condensation off the mirror. Yet as he scrubbed he became aware of an incongruous chill behind his back. Not unlike what he'd felt downstairs the night before. He glanced in the mirror. It was covered with condensation again. He felt reluctant to look round. As he turned off the tap, he heard a click. He whirled around – and saw the door had sprung open. He could have sworn he'd bolted it.

Back in the bedroom, the sight of Sandy comforted his nerves. She was already asleep, though she'd left on one of the lamps. She looked so peaceful, so alive, her skin so brown against the white sheets. He had an impulse to get in beside her. But they were narrow single beds and he really did need to catch up on sleep.

He checked the radiator was on a moderate setting, and turned in. In his sleep he dreamt he was standing under a broad carriage arch; it was night-time, and rain was spitting through the arch on the gusty wind, so the ground was muddy and the stone walls were wet. Suddenly there came a neighing, a stamping, a rattling, and big black blinkered horses burst under the arch, hooves smacking into the mud. He had to throw himself flat against the wall as they pounded past, four horses and a rain-shiny coach, a glimpse of a woman's face peering from the window, the wheels sending up spray from the puddles —

He was woken by three loud knocks and again a painful sense of urgency. He could hear a tap running. The room was very hot. What was wrong with that radiator? He looked across to Sandy's bed but couldn't make her out in the darkness. He fixed on the noise of the tap and realised the bedroom door was open.

'Sandy?'

He got up – and discovered she wasn't in bed. He went out to the corridor, flicked on the light, hurried to the bathroom. No Sandy there either; just the tap running into the basin. He switched it off and doubled back to the stairs and down to the parlour. He found her on her hands and knees, in darkness till he put on the light, her eyes open, staring, but unseeing.

'Sandy!'

No reaction. A large patch of carpet in front of her was damp, her nightdress was wet where she was kneeling on it, and between there and the front door were smaller damp patches in the shape of footprints, as of someone proceeding from the door. No time to fret about that. He had to deal with Sandy. He'd heard somewhere you shouldn't force a sleepwalker to wake up. He didn't know what to do … But now she was waking of her own accord, and weeping.

'I tried to help him!' she sobbed. 'But it was too late, he was already dying. I tried but I couldn't save him …'

'It was just a dream, honey.' He looked again at the wet patches in the carpet, whose shapes now seemed more diffuse. He put his arm round Sandy's back, so icy cold, and gently helped her upstairs.

In the morning they said nothing to each other about what had happened. As they took breakfast, Greg noticed the arched tops of the two very large windows at the front of the room.

He pointed them out to the landlord. 'Would that have been an archway once?'

'That's right; the coaches would come right through where these tables are to the stable yard.'

Greg thought about his dream. 'Can I ask you, did … er … did anything weird happen here in those days?'

'There are lots of stories about things that have happened here.' Once again that enigmatic little smile.

Sandy could see that something was on Greg's mind. 'You okay, honey?'

'I think we should get some fresh air today – blow out the cobwebs.'

They chose Cleeve Hill, because the guidebook said it was the highest point in the Cotswolds. A strong wind blew up from the Vale, but the sky was clear and from the top they could see for miles, in the west to May Hill, the Malverns and the distant Welsh mountains, and north-east past the Cotswold Edge across the wide Midland plain. Greg strode about vigorously, staring at everything as if his eyes had suddenly been opened to its glory.

'It's good to be alive!' he cried.

After all that exertion, they fell gladly into their beds that night. And again Greg dreamt – this time he was in agony from an arrow in his back, staggering through rain and biting wind, and maybe he'd done wrong but he wanted to live and if only he could get to the inn maybe someone there could save him. The building loomed out of the rain. He fell against the door and rapped his fist against it. Three loud knocks. He lurched awake, sweltering and sweaty with a searing pain in his back. He discovered the radiator was turned high again. He turned it back down. With a panic he thought of Sandy – but she was there, sprawled naked across her bed, limbs tangled in the bedclothes, hair spread like a starburst. His urge was to touch her, to caress her, but she was fast asleep. He picked up his paperback instead and went down to the bar and poured himself a whisky.

As he was carrying it to the armchair the glass dropped from his hand. Not exactly 'dropped'; it lurched out of his grip as if it had a will of its own. Whisky all over the carpet. He found a cloth and began to mop it up. The carpet was sopping. There surely couldn't have been so much liquid in the glass. In fact the soggy patch was getting bigger. Cold wetness oozed beneath his bare feet. Then he felt a familiar icy chill in the air and saw a line of wet footprints from the door.

Got to get out of this! All he could think of was Sandy. To be with her. Leaving the book forgotten on the chair, he headed for the stairs. Damp patches formed on the steps, cold on his feet, as he climbed. More of them in the corridor. From the bathroom at the end he could hear taps running. Towards that end, the corridor floor was awash with water, here lukewarm, that was seeping from under the bathroom door. Greg pushed the door open to a fug of cloud. All the taps in both basin and bath were running and water was spilling over the brims.

In the bedroom Sandy woke up boiling hot, so hot that her skin was all slippery with sweat. She pushed away the sticky bedclothes and the nightie that had somehow come off while she slept. The door opened to spill a triangle of light across the room. There was Greg in his pyjamas, his hair tufted on end as if he'd seen a ghost.

'Are you all right, Sandy?'

'Sure. You?'

'Kind of weird.' He came inside and closed the door. 'Jeez, it's hot in here! Did you turn up the radiator?'

'Not me.'

'I'll turn it down.'

'No, Greg. I like it like this.' She skated her fingertips slowly across her sweaty ribs – 'It's like being home' – and spread her arms in welcome.

Greg took off the pyjamas and lay with his wife on the bed and blessed the moist living warmth of her body against his. Later, as he lay asleep in her arms, he saw a man on a black horse burst away from the front of the inn and gallop off down the road beneath a big yellow moon. Such gladness he felt to see that horseman ride away.

Thirty

THE BEAST OF DEAN

My name is Norman and I know quite a lot about the mystery beasts of the Forest of Dean. I've spent most of my spare time keeping up to date with the sightings and I'd get down there into the field whenever I could. That the Beast is some kind of big cat is the most popular theory and the one I was inclined to believe. A viable population could have been established after the Dangerous Wild Animals Act of 1976 came into force, making it impossible for many owners to keep their exotic pets, so that many chose to release them into the wild rather than destroy them. The Forest of Dean was an obvious habitat for such animals. But exactly which species of big cat was flourishing there was unclear. That's what I wanted to find out. And to get photographs to prove it.

The latest report that spring was from a fifteen-year-old girl who'd had a close encounter on May Hill. Her name was Katrina Raywood. I contacted her mum via the school in Mitcheldean and arranged to interview the girl at their house in Ganders Green.

The mother seemed a bit wary of me, but Kat – as she called herself – was keen to tell the story of what had happened just a week before. 'I was just, like, walking in Newent Woods, near the top of May Hill, and I go past this tree which had this log or something under it. But as I passed it I saw it, like, sit up and look at me. It was a huge cat. No further away than from here to there.' She waved a hand to indicate the garden wall. 'So I carry on walking – and when I glanced back it's, like, following me. I'm really freaked out now. So I pushed through some brambles – my arms got really scratched – and legged it fast as I could till I got home.'

'You took a risk there,' I told her. 'If you run from a big cat, it can trigger the hunting instinct.'

'I was fine,' said Kat, trying to look nonchalant.

'I think it's a disgrace!' said Mrs Raywood. 'Allowing these animals to run around loose in the woods where children might be playing!'

'I'm not a child! I wasn't, like, playing.'

Kat's description of the animal was a bit vague. All we could establish was that it was big, wasn't black, and possibly had spots. We went through the pictures on my Wild Cats app, but without reaching a conclusion which species it was.

I said thanks and goodbye and, leaving my car in the village, and carrying a pack of essential kit — bivvy bag, lightweight stove, and enough dehydrated food to last forty-eight hours — I headed up the lane to Newent Woods. Before I'd even reached the woods Kat came chasing after me, a pink knapsack swinging on her shoulders.

'Let me come with you! My mum says it's okay.'

The kind of life I lead I'd never really had much to do with children — or women, to be honest. It didn't occur to me to think how others might construe the situation. I didn't really know what to say. It was Kat who took the initiative.

'Come on. I'll show you the exact place where I saw it.'

After a lot of thrashing back and forth through last year's bracken, she found the tree. A tall exotic pine. I was doubtful she could have located the right one among so many, but after a few minutes of searching the area around it I found a scat. About a week old. Bingo! I scooped it into a specimen tube.

'Eugh!' said Kat.

I positioned the girl a metre to my side and we walked in a spiral search pattern, wider and wider, till some way uphill we detected an unpleasant smell. It was from the carcass of a young roe deer with its throat ripped out.

'O my God!' cried Kat.

Now we had a vector of the animal's progress: from tree to scat to carcass. We proceeded further uphill through the bracken in that same direction, right over May Hill, and down to the southern boundary of the National Trust land. We searched up and down the fence, eyes peeled for more spoor. What we found was a section of fence that had been smashed flat. No cat, not even a lion, would have done that.

'What's this?' Kat pointed to an imprint in the muddy ground. A large cloven hoof. A cow or bull, I presumed, or a very big stag.

It was easy to follow the wake this animal had forged through the dead ferns in the wood below. It was now quite late in the afternoon. You could hear traffic droning past on the A40. Then, on a much nearer road, we heard a burst of police siren – very brief, as if just to get past another vehicle.

That siren made me think. I glanced at the girl. 'Are you sure your mum said it was all right for you to come?'

'In a way.'

'What do you mean?'

Her face turned red. 'I just, like, assumed it would be okay.'

'You mean you didn't actually ask her?'

I heard a dog barking, getting rapidly nearer. In the next few panicky moments we lost the trail we'd been following and I realised it was stupid to try to flee. We stood and waited. The dog was a huge Alsatian. It had obviously been trained to go for the man, not the girl. It cornered me against a tree, barking and snapping. Two police officers came hot on its heels – one male, one female. Kat burst into tears.

'It's all right now, love,' said the policewoman.

'I'm sorry,' sobbed Kat. 'It just seemed so cool … to try to find the Beast.'

'The Beast?' The policewoman gave me a look. 'Did he touch you?'

'Oh no! It wasn't like that.'

The policewoman led her weeping down to the car. The policeman, plus dog, stayed with me for a little chat.

'Do you like to spend time with young girls, sir?' So it began. But the man had been on the beat long enough to soon get the measure of the situation. He was just doing his job. In fact he seemed quite interested in the Beast. He didn't think it was a big cat. 'Schoolgirl's imagination, if you ask me. Wild boar – that's the Beast. A few of them escaped from farms and ran wild and now there's hundreds of the blighters. Can do a lot of damage, to gardens, crops and suchlike. Need to be culled.'

I told him about the smashed fence . 'Could a wild boar really have done that?'

'Moose-pig.'

The dog uttered a low growl.

I'd read about the moose-pig. It was supposed to be a gigantic boar that back in the 1800s had ravaged the fields near Parkend, provoking local farmers to form a posse to hunt it down.

'Not just in the 1800s,' said the policeman. 'There have been more sightings quite recently.'

Right then an unearthly roar thundered from the woods further down the hill.

'That's it!' cried the policeman. 'The moose-pig!'

The dog went berserk. It was all the man could do to restrain it.

'Didn't sound like a boar to me,' I said. 'More like an enraged bull.'

The policeman took a deep breath to calm himself. 'Well, it came from Old Moors Wood. There are fields either side, so I suppose a bull could have got in.'

'What's it like, this "Old Moors Wood"?'

'It's a wild place all right. No footpaths or anything. There are silly reports of some kind of hairy humanoid in there. An escaped gorilla, some reckon. More likely a trespassing hippie.'

It was nearly evening. The policeman had to be on his way. 'If you do find anything of a bestial nature, sir' – he handed me a card – 'do let me know and we can come and deal with it. Can't have these things wandering around causing trouble.'

Once he was gone I went straight down across the road, through Beech Grove, into Old Moors Wood. It was as wild as he'd said: dank, dark, steep; full of brambles, briars and nettles. Among the oaks and hazels was an enormous holly tree whose branches hung to the ground. Just as I was thinking that the shadowy space inside would make a good hide, a roebuck burst from a thicket, head down, ears back, and bulleted into the undergrowth. From the holly tree an arrow shot out, missing the buck – to thunk, quivering, into an oak trunk. And then from the holly branches stepped out a strange woman. Dirty blond hair in braids, a yellowish fur cloak round her shoulders, a shapeless smock, leathery bare feet and a wooden bow. She was clearly annoyed I'd startled her prey.

I apologised, and asked her if she'd seen any unusual wildlife. Her fierce green eyes regarded me as if I might be prey. She replied in a guttural language I couldn't understand; I thought maybe she was German. Giving me one more baleful look, she set off down the valley. I thought maybe she meant me to follow, so I did, though she moved so fast it was hard to keep up. The valley seemed to grow in scale the further you descended, yet remain enclosed within the wood.

Suddenly the woman broke into a run. I saw a flash of brown ahead of her – a deer, of some species larger than roe. The woman disappeared into a hazel thicket. Then stillness. Silence. As I reached the thicket an animal leapt from the trees – cleared a patch of bog in one bound. I saw it clearly: the spotted golden fur, tufted ears, bob tail. A lynx! I reached for my camera. Too late. The animal was gone.

So was the woman.

I tried, 'Hello?' Not too loud.

No sign of the woman, or the lynx, or the deer.

By now it was getting dark. I couldn't find wood dry enough to light a fire, so I lay sleepless and shivering through the night in my bivvy bag, listening to the grunts and cries of the night creatures and everywhere around me the trickling of water. In the middle of the night it rained and some of my gear got wet. Come dawn, I continued down that ever-expanding valley. All sense of the boundaries of the wood was lost. It seemed far larger than could possibly fit into the tiny area of green on the map.

I heard a noise of something large in the trees near the brook. An animal emerged into view, huge and brown, with long legs, and a long heavy snout. I didn't realise at first what it was because in this season it had no antlers. It was a bull moose, or what in Europe should be called an 'elk'. It was easily big enough to have flattened that fence. I raised my camera. The damn thing wouldn't work. Must have been the rain.

Soon the elk was gone from sight. For a time I could hear him crashing on through the trees. My mind was buzzing. If a population of elk had survived in the Forest, perhaps since prehistoric times, it could explain the legend of the moose-pig.

Yet I'd also seen a lynx, and there certainly were boar in the Forest. It seemed the 'Beast of Dean' was a composite of sightings of various different species.

I checked the camera on my phone was working. The valley lured me deeper. I had a spooky feeling the wood might yet contain more secrets, and that perhaps it wouldn't let me in so deep a second time. I continued into tougher, wilder country, beside a stream getting gradually wider, till I reached a brake of alder from which I saw a sight that made my jaw drop. It was a large boggy clearing – that was full of animals. There was a family of wild boar, the striped piglets rolling about in the mud; and a herd of five wild oxen, the cows dark brown, the bull enormous and glossy black with horns two metres across; and a pair of elk; and browsing the trees at the far side was an *elephant*, which was coated with short bristly hair as adaptation to the British climate.

Carefully I lifted my phone to take some pictures. But now the phone wouldn't work either! All I could do was gape in wonder at these creatures that once, long ago, had frequented the British wildwood.

Then I became aware of a presence behind me. Slowly I turned, to find myself face to face with a man. He was shorter than me, but enormously more powerful in build. Grizzled reddish hair grew thick on his head, chest and limbs. He wore a crude deerskin loincloth. His nose and mouth were large and jutting. Grey eyes peered intensely from the caves beneath his heavy brows. He lifted his hand. I flinched back – then realised what he'd intended, and accepted his hand. His grip was so powerful he could easily have crushed my bones. As we continued to clasp hands I felt a strange sense of communion, not only with this man, but with the animals nearby and the whole wood around us. I felt at the same time a burden of trust laid upon me.

The man let go of my hand and, without a word, strode away into the trees. I watched the animals in the clearing a while longer and then, tiredly but reluctantly, made my way back up the valley. I felt as though I was climbing out of the prehistoric past. Yet the trees, ferns, bushes, birds were no different from what you'd expect. It was only those large mammals that seemed exotic. All of them had once been part of the British ecosystem and they still would be today if they'd not been exterminated by modern man. They could conceivably become part of that ecosystem again.

My ambitions as a cryptozoologist were fulfilled beyond my wildest hopes. Except I hadn't got any photographs. That didn't really seem to matter any more. What was more important was that those animals should flourish, here in this wood, and in the rest of the Forest, and maybe someday throughout Britain. For sure, children ought to be able to play in the woods without danger, and people need to cultivate gardens and crops without them getting trashed. But can't a balance between these impulses be found? Can't the dream of true wilderness be restored in some part to this island?

BIBLIOGRAPHY

Anon., *The Mother and the Priest* (C.H. Dancey)

Anon., 'Saint Kenelm', *Eleusinianm*, online

Anon., 'Tegau Eurfron', *Nemeton*, online

Arthur, R.G. (trans.), *Three Arthurian Romances* (J.M. Dent, 1996)

Ashe, G., *Mythology of the British Isles* (Methuen, 1990)

Biquet, R., 'The Lay of the Horn', *Britannica Online Encyclopedia*

Bradshaw, J., 'St Arilda of Oldbury on Severn, Gloucestershire', *Source* No. 5, 1998 (online)

Briggs, K.M., *A Dictionary of British Folk Tales in the English Language* (Routledge & K. Paul, 1970-1)

Briggs, K.M., *The Folklore of the Cotswolds* (B.T. Batsford, 1974)

Bromwich, R. (ed.), *Trioedd Ynys Prydein* (University of Wales Press, 1978)

Child, F.J. (ed.), *The English and Scottish Popular Ballads* (Houghton, 1882-98)

Cottrell, L., *The Great Invasion* (Evans, 1958)

Doherty, P., *Isabella and the Strange Death of Edward II* (Constable, 2003)

Firstbrook, P., *The Voyage of the* Matthew (BBC, 1997)

Ford, P.K. (trans.), *The Mabinogi* (University of California Press, 1977)

Gardner, L., 'Christian Church Origins in Britain', *Golden Age Project*, 2007, online

Hartland, E.S. (ed.), *County Folklore Printed Extracts No. 1: Gloucestershire* (Folklore Society, 1895)

Hartland, E.S. (ed.), *English Fairy and Other Folk Tales* (Walter Scott, 1890)

Hudd, A.E., 'Richard Ameryk and the Name America', in *Gloucestershire Studies*, ed. H.P.R. Finberg (Leicester University Press, 1957)

Huntley, R.W., *Chavenage* (James Burns, 1845)

Jones, E.T., 'Alwyn Ruddock: John Cabot and the Discovery of America', *Historical Research*, Vol. 81, No. 212 (2008)

Jones, G., *Welsh Legends and Folk Tales* (Oxford University Press, 1955)

Leech, J., *Brief Romances from Bristol History* (William George, 1884)

Lewis-Jones, J., *Folklore of the Cotswolds* (Tempus, 2003)

Lysons, S., *Claudia and Pudens* (Hamilton, 1861)

Malmesbury, William of, *The Kings before the Norman Conquest*, trans. J. Stephenson (Seeleys, 1854)

Marshall, S., *English Folk Tales* (J.M. Dent, 1981)

Matthews, C., *Mabon and the Mysteries of Britain* (Penguin, 1987)

Matthews, J., *Secret Camelot* (Blandford, 1997)

Matthews, R., *Haunted Gloucestershire* (Logaston Press, 2006)

McKormack, T., 'The Legend of Maude's Elm', *Pagan Voice* (August 1995)

Meredith, B., *The Haunted Cotswolds* (Reardon, 1999)

Monmouth, Geoffrey of, *The History of the Kings of Britain*, trans. L. Thorpe (Penguin, 1966)

Morgan, R. W., *St Paul in Britain* (J.H. & Jas. Parker, 1861)

Musäus, J.K.A., de la Motte-Fouqué, F.H.K & Tieck, L., *Popular Tales and Romances of the Northern Nations* (W. Simpkin & R. Marshall, 1823)

Nash Ford, D., *Early British Kingdoms*, online

Newton, M., *Encyclopedia of Cryptozoology* (McFarland, 2004)

Oman, C.C., 'The English Folklore of Gervase of Tilbury', *Folklore*, Vol. 55, No. 1 (1944)

Palmer, R., *The Folklore of Gloucestershire* (Westcountry Books, 1994)

Price, J., *St Kenelm's Trail*, online

Price, M., *Folktales and Legends of Gloucestershire* (Minimax, 1984)

Ryder, T.A., *Portrait of Gloucestershire* (Robert Hale, 1972)

Sale, R., *Gloucestershire* (Crowood Press, 2002)

Sellers, Luke, 'Schoolgirl Comes Face to Face with "Black Panther" in the Forest of Dean', *This Is Gloucestershire* (2010), online

Shorey, J., *Tales of Old Bristol, Bath and Avon* (Countryside, 1989)

Smith, A., 'Lucius of Britain: Alleged King and Church Founder', *Folklore*, Vol. 90, No. 1 (1979)

Smith, B., *Tales of Old Gloucestershire* (Countryside, 1987)

St Clair Baddeley, W. , 'The Battle of Dyrham AD 577', *Transactions of the Bristol and Gloucestershire Archaeological Society*, Vol. 51 (1929)

Stevenson, R.L., *Island Nights' Entertainments* (Cassell, 1893)

Stevinson, J., *The Lives of King Kenulf of Mercia and His Family and the Legend of His Son St Kenelm* (self-published, 2005)

Stoker, B., *Famous Imposters* (Sidgwick & Jackson, 1910)

Taylor, D., 'Haunting, Folklore and Spirit Path at Lodge Park, Sherborne, Gloucestershire', *Parasearch* (2005), online

Tongue, R.L., *Forgotten Folk-Tales of the English Counties* (Routledge & K. Paul, 1970)

Turner, M., *Folklore and Mysteries of the Cotswolds* (Robert Hale, 1993)

Westwood, J., & Simpson, J., *The Lore of the Land* (Penguin, 2006)

Whitehead, J.G.O., 'Arwîrac of Glastonbury', *Folklore*, Vol. 73 (1962)

Williams, A., *Lays and Legends of Gloucestershire* (Kent, 1878)

Williams, A., *Legends, Tales, and Songs in the Dialect of the Peasantry of Gloucestershire* (Kent, 1876)

Williams, A., *Roger Plowman's Garland of Merry Tales* (Kent, 1879)

Williams, A., *Round about the Upper Thames* (Duckworth, 1922)

Williams, A.R., *Legends of the Severn Valley* (Folk Press, 1925)

Williamson, J.A., *The Cabot Voyages and Bristol Discovery under Henry VII* (Cambridge University Press, 1962)

Wilson, I., *The Columbus Myth* (Simon & Schuster, 1991)

Wright, D., 'Severn Bore, Myths and Legends', *Tidal Bore Research Society*, online